Dachshund
Handbook

D. Caroline Coile, Ph.D.

With Full-color Photographs
Illustrations by Michele Earle-Bridges

BARRON'S

Acknowledgments

Many Dachshund owners supplied information for this book, but I owe special thanks to Mary Ann Teal for her help in not only answering my questions, but in directing me to further resources. As always the staff at Barron's, led by Senior Editor and dog person extraordinaire Seymour Weiss, added their special touch to the finished product. I extend my sincere appreciation to you all.

Photo Credits

Barbara Augello, 58, 127, 129, 136, 153; Norvia Behling, 13, 33, 34 (bottom), 40, 46, 66, 88, 124, 126; Paulette Braund, vi, 22, 27, 34 (top), 36, 42, 55, 72, 77, 78, 109, 110, 113, 119, 121, 138, 148, 149, 155; Tara Darling, 3, 8, 45, 51, 59, 105, 112, 150; Kent and Donna Dannen, 5, 6, 11, 12, 14, 19 (both photos), 29, 30, 35, 43, 56, 57, 67, 70, 79, 81, 84, 87, 90, 92, 94, 95, 96, 98, 99, 102, 114, 122, 125, 130, 133, 134, 139, 143, 147, 156, 159; Shirley Fernandez, 68; Isabelle Francais, 16, 20, 23, 25, 26, 37, 50, 65, 74, 82, 111, 116, 141, 144.

About the the Author

Caroline Coile is an award-winning author who has written numerous articles about dogs for both scientific and lay publications. Her writing credits also include many well-respected books on the various aspects of dogs and dog sports. She holds a Ph.D. in neuroscience and behavior with special interests in canine sensory systems, genetics, and behavior. An active dog fancier since 1963, her own dogs have been nationally ranked in conformation, obedience, and performance activities.

Cover Photos

All cover photos are by Tara Darling.

All inquiries should be addressed to:
Barron's Educational Series, Inc.
250 Wireless Boulevard
Hauppauge, New York 11788
http://www.barronseduc.com

ISBN-13: 978-0-7641-2673-4
ISBN-10: 0-7641-2673-3

Library of Congress Catalog Card No. 2003063653

Library of Congress Cataloging-in-Publication Data
Coile, D. Caroline.
   The Dachshund handbook / D. Caroline Coile ; drawings by Michele Earle-Bridges.
      p. cm.
   Includes bibliographical references (p.).
   ISBN 0-7641-2673-3 (alk. paper)
      1. Dachshunds. I. Title.

SF429.D25C638   2004
636.753'8—dc22   2003063653

Printed in China
9 8 7

Important Note

This pet handbook gives advice to the reader on how to buy or adopt and care for a Dachshund. The author and publisher consider it important to point out that the advice given in this book applies to normally developed puppies or adult dogs acquired from recognized dog breeders or adoption sources, dogs that have been examined and are in excellent physical health with good temperament.

Anyone who adopts a fully-grown dog should be aware that the animal has already formed its basic impressions of human beings and their customary actions. The new owner should watch the animal carefully, especially its attitude and behavior toward humans. If possible, the new owner should meet the previous owner before adopting the dog. If the dog comes from a shelter, the new owner should make an effort to obtain information about the dog's background, personality, and any individual peculiarities. Dogs coming from abusive homes or from homes in which they have been treated abnormally may react to handling in an unnatural manner, and they may have a tendency to snap or bite. Such dogs should only be adopted by people experienced with handling canine behavior problems.

Caution is further advised in the association of children with dogs, both puppies and adults, and in meeting other dogs, whether on or off leash.

Even well-behaved and carefully supervised dogs sometimes do damage to someone else's property or cause accidents. It is therefore in the owner's interest to be adequately insured against such eventualities, and we strongly urge all dog owners to purchase a liability policy that covers the dog.

Contents

Chapter One

Long Ago

Hot dog, wiener dog, sausage dog, slinky dog—the Dachshund is probably the single most recognizable and nicknamed breed in the world. But that long body wasn't parked on four crooked pistons just for comic relief. It's the product of generations of selective breeding from a time when Dachshunds were better known by another name: badger dogs.

Stretching the Truth

The long and the short of Dachshund history is that everybody has a complicated theory, and nobody knows for sure. Theories of ancient origins have been advanced based on carvings of short-legged dogs from ancient Egypt, China, Greece, and South America. But it takes more than short legs to define a Dachshund. Short legs can arise by mutation in any family of dogs, and no

The heritage of a hunter, the heart of a lover...

doubt has done so repeatedly since ancient times. The Dachshund just happens to have capitalized on it more than most.

That doesn't mean Dachshunds aren't of ancient origin. Short-legged terrier-like dogs were used in ancient Rome to tangle with varmints underground. Their short legs allowed them to traverse narrow passages without sacrificing body strength. Short-legged hunting hounds were also present during the Dark Ages and Middle Ages. Their short legs allowed them to penetrate dense thickets and also kept down their pace, allowing hunters to follow them on foot. Coat types ranged from smooth to shaggy, and head types from hound-like to terrier-like. Many people believe the Dachshund originated from both hounds and terriers, inheriting the hound's trailing ability and the terrier's tenacity and inclination to go to ground.

Some of these dogs were called Dachshels, meaning badger diggers, leading some historians to assume they were early Dachshunds. More likely, Dachshel was a generic name

Short Legs

Many short-legged breeds technically have achondroplasia, a genetic condition in which the legs stop growing in length during development but continue to grow in diameter. Dachshunds have typical achrondroplastic growth plates, but they don't have the same gene responsible for achondroplasia found in some other breeds and achondroplastic humans. Some studies suggest that Dachshunds instead have chondrodysplasia, a genetic condition that results in dwarfism by causing pathological changes in the growth plates throughout the body. This may be significant because chondrodysplasia may be associated with cartilage changes that are in turn associated with intervertebral disk disease.

Cross-breeding experiments done many years ago between Dachshunds and various long-legged breeds produced offspring with legs of medium length. When bred together, the next generation had a mix of long-, medium-, and short-legged dogs, suggesting the gene that causes short legs in Dachshunds is an incomplete dominant or may be interacting with other genes.

applied to any dog that hunted badgers. Just as there is more to Dachshund conformation than stubby legs, there's more to its history than hunting badgers.

German Roots

Although the first bona fide Dachshunds emerged form Germany, nobody knows how they got there. One theory advocates that the Dachshund came to Germany from Vienna, not because of the name sausage dog, but because of the marriage of the Hapsburg heir, Maximilian, to the daughter of the Duke of Burgundy in 1477. Maximilian brought some of the Duke's many hunting hounds back to Austria, where they may have formed the basis of a superior family of hounds. Perhaps these were the Dachshund's ancestors.

Regardless of how they got there, German foresters can be credited as the true shapers of the Dachshund. The foresters needed a hardy dog that could follow a variety of quarry—rabbit, fox, badger, and even wild boar—through thick cover and even underground. The dog had to be tough enough to face a badger alone in the depths of the earth or act as one of a pack to hold a boar at bay. It had to be vocal enough to let the hunter know where it was above or below ground. It had to be small enough to fit in tight places yet strong enough to emerge victorious.

The pastime of badger hunting, in which a dog went underground to pull or flush a badger to the surface, or hold it at bay while the hunters dug to great depths for it, became popular with sportsmen in the 17th century. Confronting the European badger required courage and abilities only a few dogs could muster. Some of the best dogs incorporated the French Dachsbrake (which was in turn descended from the French Basset Hound and French Pointer) and German Dachshel. As their fame grew for hunting the badgers, they began being referred to as dachs (badger) hunds (dogs).

By the 1700s the Dachshund was clearly recognizable in various hunting and dog books. They had short legs and slender bodies and came in all colors, even white and dapple. They were said to trail and to work in burrows of badgers or foxes, and their personalities were described as "sharp," "cunning," "brave," "pugnacious," and "tenacious."

Nineteenth-century writings described the legs as "short and either crooked or straight" and colors as "yellow, brown, black, dapple,

German foresters needed a dog that could traverse varied terrain and hunt a variety of species.

and brindle." All three coat varieties were present. Interest in recording Dachshund pedigrees was rising. In 1840, the first all-breed German studbook listed 54 Dachshunds.

Badger digging required a tough dog and often considerable shoveling.

In 1848 the German Revolution placed dog breeding and badger hunting low on the list of priorities. Several pockets of Dachshund breeding persisted, and after the Revolution these dogs formed the nexus of the modern Dachshund. Once again Dachshunds took their place alongside men of leisure who enjoyed a day of hunting. It would soon take its place alongside women of leisure who enjoyed a day of competition. But that step, one of the most defining in Dachshund history, would not be made in Germany.

Blue Bloods and Blue Ribbons

The first formal dog show was held in England at Newcastle-on-Tyne in 1859. It would have enormous repercussions on dog breeds. Other shows quickly followed, encouraging the development of judging standards for as many breeds as possible. Queen Victoria's interest in dog shows made owning a purebred dog a status symbol. Dogs were imported from other countries in the rush to have the top competitors of various breeds. The Dachshund's flashy disposition and sleek silhouette made it a natural.

In 1879 a Smooth Dachshund named Feldman made a historic step when he became the first Dachshund to walk in a show ring. Within a few years, show rings were filled with Dachshunds and their owners, who

Coat Varieties

Early Dachshunds came in a variety of coat types, each best suited for particular working conditions. The long coat offered more protection and warmth than the smooth, but could get matted with mud. Some breed historians attribute the long coat to crosses with spaniels, also imparting flushing and retrieving aptitude.

The wire coat afforded the most protection against brambles. It probably came from terrier crosses, which also instilled a tougher temperament. Because of this added protection and tenacity, the Wirehaired Dachshunds were most popular with German hunters, who continued to breed them for function in favor of esthetics. The Wirehaireds were least popular with show fanciers, as the lack of attention to appearances left them lacking in points of type. In an effort to restore the Wirehaired Dachshund to the quality it once had, early German breeders resorted to careful crosses to various terriers, followed by judicious crosses back to Smooth Dachshunds to improve body type. Wirehaireds were recognized in 1890 as the third variety in Germany.

included dukes and ladies and even Queen Victoria and the Prince of Wales (later King Edward VII). With such elite backing, the world's first Dachshund Club was established in England by 1881.

Longhaired, Smooth, and Wirehaired Dachshunds each have their own advantages in the field.

The Smooth Dachshunds were the variety of choice for the English show ring for decades. Only when the Longhaired Ratzmann von Habichtscof won at Cruft's in 1923 were the Longhaireds taken seriously. Wirehaireds took even longer to gain respect.

Dog showing was also popular back in Germany. In 1888 the first German Dachshund standard was approved. It would be seven more years before the German club, the Deutche Teckel Klub, was established. Dachshunds became one of Germany's most popular pets and successful show dogs, without sacrificing their hunting heritage. But don't call them Dachshunds in Germany; there they are known as Teckels.

The Dachshund Conquers America

The first Dachshunds in the New World probably accompanied German or English immigrants. Dachshunds were exhibited in American Kennel Club (AKC) dog shows even before the first Dachshund—a dog named Dash—was AKC registered in 1885. Interest and numbers grew, leading to the formation of the Dachshund Club of America (DCA) in 1895. By 1913 the Dachshund had become a popular show dog, even boasting one of the Westminster Kennel Club's largest entries. The Dachshund's future looked bright.

World War I changed everything. The Dachshund's recognition as national dog of the Teutonic Empire in Europe bode poorly of its future in America, where everything German

Dachshunds have always been ready to go anywhere and fit in any lifestyle.

became the object of persecution. Only a few Dachshund breeders could afford, financially and socially, to keep their dogs. The AKC tried to help by changing the breed's name to Badger Dog in 1919. By the time the name was changed back to Dachshund in 1923 only 26 new Dachshunds were registered that year. If the Dachshund were a species, it would be on the endangered list.

But Dachshunds had made new friends during the war. They beguiled American servicemen into taking them home from Germany. Although most of these dogs could not be integrated into the breeding stock because of confusion over their Ger-

man registration status, they played an even more valuable role as Dachshund ambassadors. With growing popularity and replenished stock from Europe, Dachshunds were proving you can't keep a good dog down, no matter how short it was.

Back in the show ring, they met all comers. Dachshunds were shown in the Working group during much of the 1920s, then spent two years in the Sporting group, and finally found their home in the Hound group in 1931. They may be the only breed to win all three groups.

During this period Champion (Ch.) Kensal's Call Boy won the first Best in Show for the breed. In the late 1930s, Ch. Herman Rinkton attracted worldwide attention with his record-setting 14 Best in Shows. Whereas Call Boy and Herman influenced Dachshund history with their show records, it was Ch. Favorite von Marienlust that influenced it even more as a producer. Favorite sired 95 champions; his son and grandson held the second and third place stud records siring 90 and 82 champions each, respectively.

The Dachshund show scene in America was ruled by the standard Smooths for many years. Although a few Longhaireds had been kept as pets, only in 1931 was the first Longhaired, named Beauty, registered with the AKC. The first Longhaired champion, Kobold v Fuchenstein, competed against Smooths. The 1940s saw the first Longhaired Best in Show winner, Ch. Antonio of Gypsy Barn.

Weights and Measures

Dachshunds come in different sizes for a reason. Hunting badgers or boars required strong Dachshunds that often weighed over 30 pounds. Trailing wounded deer or hunting foxes required slightly smaller Dachshunds (perhaps around 15 to 20 pounds) that could squirm through thickets or into a den. Dachshunds that specialized in hunting rabbits needed to be smaller still, weighing well under 10 pounds.

Some small Dachshunds were just naturally occurring smaller dogs, sometimes called Zwerg (dwarf) Dachshunds. Others resulted from purposefully breeding smaller Dachshunds together. These dogs were Kaninchenteckels. Some breeders crossed Dachshunds with various toy dogs, creating small round-headed dogs with various non-Dachshund traits. These were called Kaninchenhundes. Show fanciers and pet owners clamored for the minis. By 1902, eleven miniature Dachshunds were registered in Germany.

Although the Kaninchenhundes made good companions, they could not compete against the other types of minis in the show ring. Without the backing of the show fancy, the Kaninchenhundes disappeared after a couple of decades.

The Kaninchenteckel fared better. A few went to England after World War I, but not until after World War II was a concerted effort made to breed quality miniatures. In 1948 some of the best of these dogs came to America. They did well at dog shows, but their real claim to fame was their visibility as media stars, sharing the spotlight with Bob Hope in the movie *Fancy Pants* and with Dennis Day and Ray Bolger on their television shows. Despite such exposure the miniatures still had to fight their way to show wins. Only in the 1960s did their popularity take off.

One size may not fit all, but three come close.

7

The Dachshund Becomes a Hot Dog

The Dachshund's popularity as a show dog was eventually eclipsed by its popularity as a pet. The breed's distinctive and sometimes comical look made it a natural attention-getter, and to know a Dachshund was to want one. By 1940, the Dachshund had risen to sixth amongst all breeds in popularity, and it has continued as one of America's, and the world's, most popular breeds since.

A little popularity is good. A lot of popularity is not—at least, not for a dog breed. As Dachshund numbers soared, more people felt the urge to breed their dogs. Not every Dachshund had the temperament, health, or physical qualities that exemplified the breed. Yet these dogs were bred repeatedly, with no regard for the quality of the dogs produced or the lives they lived. Dogs with improper socialization, poor temperaments, and poor health were sold to people who didn't know the difference, and who in turn bred their poor-quality Dachshunds. As numbers grew and quality fell, prices also fell, and more people got Dachshunds on a whim, only to abandon them at the slightest problem. Today Dachshund rescue groups fight a never-ending tide of unwanted Dachshunds, victims of their own popularity.

Of course, there's a reason they're so popular.

The Dachshund is a breed forever reaching new heights.

The early history of the Wirehaired variety in America is obscure. It wasn't until the 1940s that they were imported and shown in any great numbers. Best in Show winner Ch. Brentwald of Joshua was the first Wirehaired to dominate the show rings.

While Dachshunds continued to prosper at American dog shows, there were few chances for them to prove themselves in the field. The institution of field trials by the AKC in 1935 was a significant step in maintaining hunting ability in the breed.

Chapter Two

Dachshund Demeanor and Design

The Dachshund's hunting heritage shaped a dog as distinctive in personality as in appearance. Today's Dachshund more typically hunts for morsels under the table than for varmints underground, but he retains the conformation and temperament of a hunter. To ignore these traits so integral to his being is to ignore his very soul.

True to Form

Dachshunds have the most distinctive silhouette in dogdom, one that has elicited the overused descriptions of hot dog and wiener dog, as well as the more imaginative bumper sticker that urges us to "Get a long little doggy." Despite the esthetic or even comedic aspects of their structure, the Dachshund's dimensions have their basis in hunting ability.

Confronting a badger, which can only be described as 35 pounds of fury in a hole, requires a dog with a strong supple body. The Dachshund's dwarfed legs allow the greatest combination of strength and short

stature needed to traverse narrow burrows. The chest must be large enough to accommodate good-sized lungs and heart, yet not so large that it impedes the dog's ability to squeeze through tight places. Adding body length rather than depth helps the dog meet these requirements.

Standard Dachshunds are heavier than they look, usually weighing from 16 to 32 pounds. Miniature Dachshunds, weighing up to 11 pounds, were bred to trail wounded game or hunt rabbits or foxes. No matter what the size, the Dachshund should be muscular, not just for the sake of being correct for the hunt, but for maintaining a healthy body.

The Dachshund's low-slung keel is another go-to-ground adaptation. When the Dachshund is called upon to do some serious digging, he can rest his front end on his deep chest and free both front legs for digging. Carried to an extreme, however, the keel can take up too much valuable maneuvering room.

Squeezing through a tight burrow requires not only short legs, but well-formed ones. The angle formed between the shoulder blade and

Sizing Up the Dachshund

The AKC recognizes two sizes of Dachshunds: the familiar standard and the increasingly popular miniature. The standard weighs between 16 and 32 pounds, while the miniature weighs under 11 pounds as an adult. That leaves some dogs in between, and Dachshunds weighing between 11 and 16 pounds are affectionately called "tweenies."

Other parts of the world do things differently. A few countries categorize sizes by torso length. In the Dachshund's homeland of Germany, the circumference of the rib cage just under the elbows determines size. A dog with chest circumference measuring over 35 centimeters (13.8 inches) is a standard, and one with a circumference of 30 to 35 centimeters (11.8 to 13.8 inches) is a miniature. In addition, an even smaller size, called kaninchen, measures less than 30 centimeters (11.8 inches) in chest circumference.

upper arm appears as almost 90 degrees, allowing the dog to fold its legs tighter to its body. Not only does this afford the freest movement within a burrow, but also the most efficient movement—given the short legs—when traveling between burrows. The single disqualification in the AKC Dachshund standard is knuckling over of the front legs, a condition in which the wrist joint appears to be in front of the pasterns.

Hunting pressures also helped shape the Dachshund's expression. The strong jaws required to grip his quarry requires a wide flare alongside the skull and a long backskull to afford a route and attachment point for jaw muscles. The jaw contains a full set of large teeth that meet in a punishing scissors bite. The Dachshund's eye opening must be fairly small in order to better protect the eye, but it cannot be so small that it encourages ocular problems.

From the tip of his nose with its acute sense of smell to the tip of its wagging tail, the Dachshund's physique was formed by generations of hunting. His psyche was just as much affected.

Doxie Moxie

Generations of selection for a bold, energetic, inquisitive, and relentless hunting dog produced a strong-willed dog that has his own ideas about how to best function as your companion. Don't get a Dachshund and expect to mold him to your ideals if they go against what his genes tell him; he will win any battle of the wills. Remember, a badger hunter must

• Make its own decisions when deep underground. He must be independent and self-directed—even when his owner commands otherwise.

• Be tenacious in the face of adversity—even if that adversity is being told *"No!"*

Dachshunds have the most distinctive silhouette in dogdom (miniature black and tan Smooth).

• Bark with vigor and stamina—much to the neighbor's dismay.
• Solve problems—even if that problem is how to escape from the yard.
• Harass quarry—much to your cat's disgust.
• Be anxious to go underground—even if that means getting stuck under the porch and riddling the yard with holes.

Fortunately, the Dachshund is as consummate a companion as he is a hunter. He is loving, snuggly, compassionate, playful, witty, smart, and comes with a nonstop sense of humor—traits that make Dachshund lovers overlook almost any Dachshund misdoings.

Dachshunds as Companions

Although a few people still hunt with their Dachshunds, and many people compete with them in conformation and performance events, most Dachshund owners simply value their dogs as companions. Dachshunds aren't for everybody; before taking the plunge into Dachshund ownership consider these common questions about the breed.

Are Dachshunds hard to train? Think again what the Dachshund was bred to do. He used his own wits to seek out game, follow it underground far away from his human partners, decide how best to tackle his opponent, and confront a badger head on. What about his heritage would lead you to believe he is anxiously awaiting your commands? Today's Dachshunds, like their ancestors, investigate and think for themselves. Some people call that smart; others call it mischievous. They don't give up just because they meet with opposition. Some people call that tenacious; others call it stubborn. The gist of it is that Dachshunds are not jump-to-it, tell-me-what-to-do-next, I'm-your-obedient-servant type dogs. Once

The Dachshund's body can squeeze through places no other dog would dream of entering (standard Longhaired puppy).

when forced to do something, they dig in the dirt until your yard is stippled with pockmarks. They bark. They bark a lot. They bark at burglars, but some also bark at squirrels, falling leaves, and passing traffic. Some may try to protect your belongings from those burglars, chomping ferociously at their calves; others will concentrate on leading them to your refrigerator for a shared snack. A few Dachshunds are indiscriminate in their protection duties, gleefully nipping anyone who visits. But all Dachshunds became stalwart defenders when their special people are threatened. They will hurl threats and do what they can to scare away those who might accost their loved ones.

Dachshunds like to hunt, and will usually consider the world beyond your yard fertile hunting grounds. They will dig, squeeze, and squirm their way through weak areas in your fence and, once free, will follow their noses. Sometimes they forget to come back.

Housetraining can be a challenge. In fact, lack of housetraining is one of the main reasons Dachshunds are placed in rescue. You can do your best to avoid this problem by following the instructions on page 34. Separation anxiety can be a particular problem in the breed, leading to home destruction and, sadly, to permanent separation when the owner places the dog in rescue. This, too, is avoidable (see page 64). Other problems can be prevented with proper choice, socialization, and training.

you show them how to do something, they will think of all the other ways it can be done more imaginatively. Once you put up roadblocks or add corrections, they will see it as a challenge to their determination. But Dachshunds have a soft spot—a few, really. They love to have fun, they love to eat, and they love to be loved. Training with fun methods and positive reinforcement has produced some phenomenally responsive Dachshunds. Dachshunds can put their minds toward good deeds as long as you make it worth their while.

Do Dachshunds have personality quirks? Dachshunds aren't perfect. Besides digging in their heels

Are Dachshunds good with children? Dachshunds and children can form close friendships, but the Dachshund is not the ideal dog for a young child. Dachshunds tend to be stubborn when it comes to being pushed around, and may not tolerate blatantly unfair treatment. If the dog cannot find refuge from rough handling, he could snap in self-defense. An overly tolerant Dachshund is at risk of back injuries. Older children who are gentle and responsible are the best match; they can play for hours with a frisky Dachshund.

Too many new parents replace their Dachshund, who was once the baby of the family, with their new human baby. They banish the dog to the yard or take him to the shelter because they fear the dog will hurt the baby or they don't have time to divide their attention. There's no reason to do this. While no dog should ever be left unsupervised with a young child or baby, Dachshunds and children can relate like siblings. Don't get a Dachshund as a stopgap measure before you have a baby. Get a Dachshund for life, or don't get one at all.

Are Dachshunds good with other pets? Dachshunds get along well with other dogs, particularly other Dachshunds. If you spend a lot of time away from home, your Dachshund will be happier with a canine buddy. Having another dog will not diminish your dog's love for you and may help with problems such as separation anxiety. If the other dog is much larger, you will need to take

Children and Dachshunds can be the best of friends.

precautions so he doesn't hurt your Dachshund in overzealous play. Two dogs of the opposite sex usually get along better, and spaying and neutering also helps keep the peace.

If raised with cats, Dachshunds can be great pals with them. An older Dachshund may or may not adapt to feline friendship. The Dachshund's hunting heritage makes camaraderie with rodents less likely, and adding a pet badger to your household is especially ill advised.

Are Dachshunds difficult to care for? Keeping a Dachshund is no more difficult than caring for any other royal personage. Any worthy

Dachshunds can be thrill-seekers (miniature Smooth).

Dachshund hand-servant will provide a couple of small tasty and nutritious meals a day, a snuggly bed, regular grooming, veterinary care, exercise, attention, and 100 percent devotion.

Feeding is not an expensive proposition because Dachshunds don't require much food. The challenge is keeping their bodies sausage shaped instead of stuffed sausage shaped. Feeding a Dachshund means developing resistance to the patented *"I'd love you even more if you fed me more treats"* Dachshund expression.

Bedding should be soft and easily accessible without jumping. Their favorite sleeping spot is wherever your favorite sitting or sleeping spots are. If you wish to share, make a Dachshund ramp or stairway so your dog doesn't have to jump up and down. Smooths, especially, are heat-seeking missiles who use their burrowing talents to crawl under the bedcovers, making a handy substitute for a hot water bottle! If you prefer separate beds make sure your Dachshund's sleeping quarters are close enough to the hub of household activity that the dog doesn't feel isolated. Dachshunds are social animals and they will not be happy banished to the garage. They are definitely not outdoor sleepers; although they relish the chance to play in the yard, they are not designed to sleep outside. None of the Dachshund coat types is sufficient to insulate them from extreme cold or excessive heat.

Grooming depends on coat type. Smooths require only a few weekly swipes of the brush and an occasional bath. Long coats need combing a few times a week to prevent tangling and matting. Wire coats also require combing a couple of times a week unless you want a show coat, which requires more effort. Check out the section on grooming (page 49) for more details on just how much work is involved. Dachshunds are not plagued by doggy odor.

Exercise is essential. Dachshunds are get-up-and-go dogs that need to burn off excess energy and stretch their legs and mind. They need an invigorating patrol around the neighborhood or a pantingly fun game at home every day. Giving a Dachshund's short legs a workout is not too difficult, but keeping a Dachshund's mind occupied can be challenging. Dachshunds live a perpetual quest for adventure. Their ancestors quivered to go on search and destroy missions after wild vermin, and the genes of modern Dachshunds propel them to do the same. Their genes tell them to roam, hunt, explore, chase, and mangle whenever the chance arises. If they can't do it outside, they will do it inside, killing toys and amusing their family with their antics—or shredding heirlooms and dismaying their family with their dastardly deeds. The moral: exercise a Dachshund's body and mind, or prepare to exercise your self-control.

Attention is a Dachshund's lifeblood. They crave affection, and they blossom when they are the object of all eyes. They won't hesitate to put on a floorshow to entertain the family, or squiggle into a lap to soak up love. They are exuberant in their affections, and will wilt if they cannot be with their loved ones. Don't get a Dachshund if you don't plan on your dog being a real and actively participating member of your family.

Are Dachshunds healthy? Dachshunds are generally long lived, easily reaching their mid-teens. Nonetheless, as with any dog, veterinary care can be a major expense. Routine care, such as check-ups, heartworm prevention, vaccinations, and neutering or spaying, can tax tight budgets. Plan for a few bouts of more expensive nonroutine care during your dog's lifetime.

Dachshunds have a few minor health concerns, and one that is serious and breed-related. The serious one, intervertebral disc disease, affects as many as one in four Dachshunds. You can minimize the probability by keeping your Dachshund trim and fit and by preventing your Dachshund from excessive jumping. See page 128 for more information.

Dachshunds are loving and fun-loving dogs in search of loving and fun-loving people. If that's you, your next step is to find your own Dachshund dear.

Chapter Three

Dachshund Decisions

Dachshunds have burrowed into the hearts of people around the world. They've done this with a mischievous sense of humor and a loving sense of family few other breeds can challenge—and they've done so in a medley of alluring coats, colors, and sizes. Choosing the Dachshund as your breed was the easy part; choosing which Dachshund will be yours is far more daunting!

Dachshund Options

Dachshunds come in an unparalleled assortment of sizes, coat types, and colors, each with special appeal.

Sizing Up the Dachshund

Your choice of size has some practical implications. If you want your dog to be a hiking companion, a standard Dachshund is a better choice. A standard Dachshund is also preferable for a home with children or other large dogs, as they are slightly more resis-

Dachshunds need to get outside and enjoy nature.

tant to injury. If you like a dog to hold and cuddle, a miniature Dachshund will be better suited. The tiny kaninchenteckels, bred for rabbit hunting, are not popular in the United States, but also make endearing and handy companions.

Tweenies have all the wonderful attributes of the other sizes, but can't compete as miniatures and can't compete successfully as standards in the show ring. That means that show breeders often have tweenies available as pets that are every bit as well-bred and beautiful as their top show specimen littermates.

The Long and the Short— and the Wire—of It

The familiar Dachshund most of us grew up with had a short sleek coat, perfect for stroking. But Dachshunds also come in a voluptuous long coat and a dapper wire coat. Their differences may be more than fur, or even skin, deep. Because they derived from different ancestors, the three coat types tend to have slightly different personalities. All are first and foremost Dachshunds in temperament. But Smooths tend to be more one-person or one-family dogs, remaining fairly aloof with strangers. Longhaireds are the lovers, described as the sweetest members of the breed. Wirehaireds are the clowns of the bunch, tending to be more extroverted. Grooming any of the coats is not difficult. The Smooths should be brushed once a week. The long coats should be combed once or twice a week, and perhaps trimmed occasionally. Wire coats can be combed weekly, but need to have the old dead hair plucked out twice a year. Without this care, some wire coats tend to grow long and soft, creating a tumbleweed effect.

A Dox of a Different Color

For many people, if it's not red or perhaps black and tan, it can't be a Dachshund. But the Dachshund palette is one of the most colorful of all dogs. True, color should be low on the list of criteria when choosing a new friend, but all else being equal, why not get the color you find most esthetically pleasing?

Traditionalists may still opt for a fiery red or flashy black and tan, but those with more exotic tastes might prefer a pied, brindle, dapple, or cream. Dachshund colors are:

• *Red:* Reds can range from chestnut to deep mahogany. They may be clear reds or black-fringed reds, often with a slight black overlay. The black fringing may only be noticeable in the long coats, where it is seen on the ear tips.

• *Cream:* Creams are buff colored, ranging from a light tan to yellowish beige. Most creams in America are really dilute reds. Such dogs often have a lighter nose color. True creams, which come mostly from English lines, have dark noses.

• *Wheaten:* Wheatens fill the gap between reds and creams, but don't have as homogenous coloration as either. Wheaten is a color more typically seen in wire coats.

• *Wild Boar:* Wild boars are the color of wild boars: a grizzled mixture of gray, brown, and black, with each hair banded with several shades. It is a color typically seen in wire coats.

• *Red Boar:* Red boars are wild boars with a red hue.

• *Sable:* In most breeds sables are dogs with black hairs interspersed among their base color (most often red) hairs. In Dachshunds the desig-

The Longhaired Dachshund has a dramatic beauty (standard Longhaired).

The Smooth Dachshund has a sleek elegance (miniature Smooth).

nation of sable is reserved for dogs with black- (or dark-) tipped hairs. Such dogs may appear almost black until the coat is parted and the lighter part of the hair is seen near the base. The shorter hair of the face and legs is typically lighter.

• *Black and Tan:* Black and tans are tan-pointed dogs with a black base color. Tan pointed means they have tan on the muzzle, eyebrows, feet, part way up the legs, and under the tail. The extent of tan markings can vary widely, with some dogs having hardly any. The tan points may range from rich red to creamy beige, preferably without black smudging.

• *Chocolate and Tan:* Chocolate dogs have brown where the black would be on a black and tan. The

The Wirehaired Dachshund has a saucy sophistication (wheaten colored Wirehaired).

brown ranges from milk chocolate to dark chocolate in shade. Chocolate dogs always have brown, instead of black, eye rims and nose. Their eyes are typically lighter in color.

• *Blue and Tan:* Blue and tans have gray where the black would be on a black and tan. The gray ranges from slate gray to light, almost bluish, gray but is most often described as pewter gray. Blue dogs always have gray, instead of black, noses and eye rims. Blue dogs of many breeds are prone to certain coat and skin problems.

• *Fawn and Tan (Isabella):* Isabellas have a silvery fawn color, similar to the Weimaraner's coat color, where the black would be on a black and tan. They have lighter colored nose, eye rims, and eye color. Because they result from a dog that is both chocolate and blue, they are prone to the same coat and skin problems as are blue dogs.

• *Brindle:* Brindles have irregular dark stripes superimposed over their base coat color. The stripes are usually black, but can also be chocolate or, rarely, gray or fawn (Isabella). When a tan-pointed dog is also brindled, the brindle stripes are visible only on the tan parts. Brindles must have at least one brindle parent.

• *Piebald:* Piebalds are spotted with areas of full color over a white background. The color that peeps through the white retains whatever its underlying pattern is, so it may be red, black and tan, brindle, dapple, or any other base color. Ticking, small dots of full color, may or may not be present. Piebald is not specifically mentioned in the AKC standard, but it is a traditional color and acceptable in AKC shows. However, most European countries do not allow piebalds to be shown.

• *Dapple:* Dapples are a pattern better known as merle in other breeds, in which lighter areas are intermingled with darker areas of coloration. It can be superimposed over any base color, such as red, black and tan,

The Double Dapple Dilemma

Among the Dachshund's flashiest color patterns is the double dapple, which combines wild marbling with bright white highlights. When everything goes right, it is stunning. But when things go wrong, it can be heartbreaking. Some show breeders produce double dapples in an attempt to get a flashy show dog. They do this knowing they must carefully evaluate all the double dapples for visual or auditory problems, and take responsibility for any compromised puppies. Some commercial breeders produce them because buyers are attracted to them. They do this with little concern about problems that may not be obvious at the time of sale. Some naive breeders produce them because they don't know any better. They often think that by breeding two dapples together they will get more dapples. In fact, on average half of the litter will be dapples, one quarter will be non-dapples, and one quarter will be double dapples. Some well-intentioned breeders inadvertently breed two dapples together because occasionally a dapple will have so few patches of mottled coloration it appears undappled. If even a single tiny patch of mottled hair is visible at any time of the dog's development, especially if that dog had a dapple parent, the dog is still genetically dapple. Since extent of dappling is random rather than hereditary, such a dog has just as great a chance of producing double dapples with large areas of white as do parents that are extensively dappled. By the same token, double dapples will sometimes be difficult to tell from dapples because not all double dapples have white areas.

Don't confuse a piebald with a double dapple. Piebalds almost always have a white tail tip and seldom have blue or blue-flecked eyes. Of course, a piebald dapple is difficult to tell from a double dapple.

If your heart is set on a double dapple, contact a responsible breeder who is known for producing them. Make sure the puppy's vision and hearing are checked by a veterinarian before you accept it. It's possible to share a fulfilling life with a blind or deaf dog, or even a blind and deaf dog, but it's not fair for you to first fall in love with a puppy and then find out it has unanticipated special needs.

chocolate and tan, and blue and tan. Dappling can be hard to discern when the base color is already light. The extent and distribution of dappling appears to be random. In some cases it is so extensive that it's hard to tell what the fully pigmented base color is; in others, it can be so restricted that without close scrutiny the dog appears undappled. One or both eyes may be blue or blue flecked.

Dapples occur in a wide range of coloration. Double dapples have a great deal of white sometimes, like the dog on the left.

• *Double Dapple:* Double dapples occur when two dapples are bred together; the progeny with two copies of the dapple gene have dappling and usually some areas of white. These white areas seem to be where the pigment-removing influence of both genes is exerted, and like dapples, their extent and distribution is random. This is the problem. If the double dappling occurs in the eyes or ears, the dog will have visual or auditory problems, very often being totally deaf or blind or both. Some dogs have abnormally small or even missing eyes. Compared to other breeds in which "double dappling" occurs (albeit by a different name), Dachshunds seem to have fewer and less severe visual and auditory problems.

Color Cautions

With all these colors and patterns, Dachshunds can come in a smorgasbord of combinations. You can imagine a cream brindle pied, or a double dapple Isabella. But good Dachshunds seldom come in weird combinations. Dachshund breeders who breed for good conformation, good health, and good temperament usually find themselves working with the large gene pools represented by the more common colors. Breeders who concentrate on interbreeding less common colors among themselves may be sacrificing more

A dapple Wire puppy.

important traits by limiting their available gene pools. Commercial or naive breeders may focus on unusual combinations because they can give them exotic names, advertise them as rare, and ask higher prices for them. No Dachshund color is exotic or rare; some are less common than others, but none should command a higher price.

Be aware that certain colors may be associated with certain health problems. Double dapples may have visual or auditory problems. Blues and, to a greater extent, Isabellas, often have a skin condition called color dilution alopecia, in which the hair is sparse. Pies with extensive white have a greater probability of being deaf, especially if the white is around the ears. And despite the wide range of allowable colors, not everything is acceptable from the point of view of the standard. Pure black or pure chocolate Dachshunds occasionally occur, but are not considered correct. Dapple piebalds are difficult to tell from double dapples. If both parents are dapples, they are probably double dapples. Pies are only acceptable for showing in certain countries. Because the AKC only records one pattern per dog, it is impossible to trace colors of multi-patterned dogs with any accuracy if you are relying on AKC-certified pedigrees. Some colors are considered mismarks. A dog with a white blaze

Well-bred and raised Dachshunds are not cheap. Although a dog from a responsible breeder may seem expensive compared to one from a backyard breeder, consider what has gone into the production of this pup. The parents may have health clearances, which entailed some expense. They probably have conformation championships and perhaps obedience or other performance titles, which cost the breeder a lot of money, time, and effort to earn. They themselves were bought at considerable expense because their parents in turn had health clearances and titles. The breeder probably paid a stud fee and possibly shipping fees to breed to the best male available rather than to the closest one. Prebreeding health tests, ovulation testing, and prenatal care (which may include fetal monitoring, radiographs, and ultrasound) can be costly, as can a Caesarian section. The breeder may take time off work to monitor the whelping and care for the newborns. Responsible breeders make many sacrifices to produce quality Dachshunds; their commitment doesn't end when you walk out the door. You're not just buying a better puppy; you're buying a pup with the best start possible in life, and you're buying the breeder's advice for the duration of that pup's life.

Don't confuse price with quality. Unscrupulous puppy mills invest as little as they can in their pups, in turn wholesaling them to retailers who charge top dollar.

or a white chest is mismarked, not pied. A dog with such dark tan on its points that the dog appears solid black or chocolate is also considered mismarked. While these dogs make equally beautiful companions, they should not be sold as exotic or rare.

The same caveats are true of other Dachshund variables. Many commercial breeders interbreed all sizes, coat types, and colors in an effort to produce unusual combinations. Be suspicious of breeders who advertise their Dachshunds as rare or exotic. They should be advertising them as healthy and sound of body and mind. There's nothing wrong with wanting a favorite color, size, or coat type, but don't let that become your priority.

Looking for Trouble

Dachshund puppies are readily available through newspaper ads, pet stores, bulletin boards, and web sites. Although you can get a wonderful companion from any of these sources, better sources are available. Most people who advertise in newspapers or on bulletin boards breed a litter because they think it will be exciting, because somebody told them their dog was beautiful, or because they want to give the children an opportunity to witness the miracle of birth, to make a few extra dollars, or to get another dog just like the mom. They neglect to learn about Dachshund health problems, pedigrees, structure, or socialization, so the health, conformation, and temperament of the pups is largely a matter of chance.

Large-scale commercial Dachshund breeders, also known as puppy mills, are in it strictly for the money. The problem is, dog breeding isn't particularly lucrative unless you cut corners. So they churn out puppies as fast as they can, keep lots of dogs in tiny cages, provide minimal care and cheap food, and breed them every season regardless of any health, temperament, or conformation problems. Avoid any breeder who has many litters available, has litters from several breeds, sells whole litters at a time, won't let you visit the premises, or can get you any combination of coat and color you desire. The pups from these breeders have the scales tipped against them. Some of these unethical breeders are sophisticated enough to know what a good breeder should look like; they field calls for a number of breeds and then hustle one of their many litters to a home to pose as family-raised pups. Check out ads for other breeds and if the phone numbers match, avoid them.

Responsible Breeders

Breeders who focus on breeding quality Dachshunds are the best choice if you want the best Dachshund. Responsible breeders, sometimes called hobby breeders, prove their dogs in some form of competition and screen them for hereditary health problems. Nonetheless, not every pup will turn out to be competition quality. Some will have slight imperfections that only a breed authority could notice. Some may be tweenies, and so not be suitable for a successful show career. And many breeders will sell a competition-quality dog as a pet simply because finding the best home for that dog outweighs its show career. Pet-quality pups will have profited from the breeder's knowledge of genetics and puppy care, and they need loving homes. Responsible breeders will expect you to keep them abreast of your pup's progress and come to

Black and tan Smooth puppies.

A cream Longhaired Dachshund says hello.

them with their problems for the duration of your Dachshund's life.

Responsible breeders can be located through Dachshund clubs, dog magazines (especially Dachshund magazines), or kennel pages on the Internet. Be wary of Internet listings, which are often placed by commercial or unscrupulous breeders. A good place to find good breeders is at a dog show or, even better, a Dachshund specialty show (a prestigious show in which only Dachshunds compete). The annual Dachshund Club of America national specialty is the premier Dachshund event in America. It attracts hundreds of top competitors in conformation and performance events. Not only can you meet more good breeders at

large specialties, but you can also get a better idea of what traits are most important to you. Dachshund clubs are another good source of breeder referrals. The Dachshund Club of America web site lists contacts for every regional Dachshund Club in the United States. It also offers a breeder referral listing members who adhere to the club's code of ethics.

Talking to prospective breeders is only the first step. Visit them personally and see for yourself how the adults look and act, and how puppies are being raised. Every breeder should meet the following criteria:

• Raises puppies in the home, not in a kennel building or garage.

• Has puppies and adults that seem acclimated to living as part of the family, rather than in cages or pens.

• Has outgoing, confident adults and puppies with temperaments you like.

• Has clean, well-groomed, healthy-appearing dogs.

• Is familiar with and screens for Dachshund health concerns.

• Can compare the parents to the breed standard feature by feature.

• Charges neither bargain basement nor exorbitant prices.

• Has the mother of the litter available to meet.

• Has photos and pedigrees of both parents and other relatives.

• Has registration papers available at the time of purchase.

• Breeds sparingly and dedicates breeding efforts to only one or two breeds.

• Belongs to a local and/or national Dachshund club.

Look to the parents for a preview of your puppy as an adult—but also keep in mind each is an individual.

- Is involved in some sort of Dachshund competition.
- Asks you lots of questions about your past history with dogs, facilities, family, life-style, and expectations for your new dog.
- Can tell you how puppies from former litters are doing and provide references from former puppy buyers.
- Won't allow puppies to leave until they are at least 8 or preferably 10 weeks old.
- Does not require puppy-back agreements that require you to breed the dog. Doesn't pressure you into buying a pup, especially if you've asked to think about it first.
- Requires that should you ever have to relinquish the dog she gets first refusal.
- Provides a medical history, pedigree, registration information, and written care instructions with each puppy.
- Agrees the sale is contingent on you having your veterinarian check the puppy within the first two days you have it.

Ask about the health of your prospective puppy's relatives, and the cause of death of any deceased ancestors. Any problems that appear on the list of Dachshund genetic diseases (see page 120) should be investigated further.

Puppy Picking

Good breeders have waiting lists for their puppies before they breed a litter. That means you may have to wait several months to get the puppy of your dreams. Even then, the breeder may be the one choosing your future friend. A responsible

Puppy Health Checklist

- *Behavior:* look out for shyness, sharpness, crying, or lethargy and for coughing, sneezing, vomiting, or diarrhea.
- *Hydration:* look out for skin that doesn't pop back into place after being lifted away from the body on the back. Lack of elasticity indicates dehydration, often from illness.
- *Coat:* check for thinning or missing hair, crusted or reddened skin, or signs of parasites such as the black "flea dirt" that turns red upon getting wet.
- *Eyes:* look out for unusually small size, squinting, discharge, tearing, redness, or cloudiness. The lids should not be rolled inward so they irritate the cornea.
- *Ears:* look out for redness, swelling, or dirtiness in the canal, bad odor, or repeated head shaking or head tilting.
- *Nose:* look out for crustiness or mucous discharge, which could indicate illness.
- *Gums:* look out for pale gums, which may indicate anemia.
- *Teeth:* look out for misaligned teeth, or for an upper jaw that overshoots the lower one significantly, such that you could place a finger in the gap. The lower canine teeth (fangs) should be in front of the upper canine teeth when the pup's mouth is closed.
- *Limbs:* look out for limping or for limbs that do not match.
- *Torso:* check for a potbelly or excessive thinness, which could indicate internal parasites.
- *Anus:* look out for redness or irritation, which indicates diarrhea.
- *Testicles:* feel for two small testicles in the scrotum, which should be present in males by 8 to 12 weeks of age. If not descended by then, chances are they never will. Undescended testicles render a dog ineligible for conformation shows and, unless surgically removed, are more prone to becoming cancerous.

breeder knows the puppies' personalities and will make sure you get the best match for your needs. You may get to choose from among several puppies, though, so be prepared to choose with both your brain and your heart.

Dachshund puppies should be playful, curious, alert, and self-confident. Choose neither the boldest nor shyest puppy. A puppy that cringes, freezes, or always heads home when carried away from her littermates may not have the self-confidence of the typical Dachshund. One that growls or snaps in a nonplayful manner is best left for an expert to handle. Give extra points to the puppy who picks you by crawling in your lap or crowding into the way when you're trying to look at the others!

Age of Consent

Responsible Dachshund breeders won't place pups until they are at least 8 or even 10 weeks of age. Small puppies are more vulnerable to the stress of changing homes, so miniatures may need to stay with the breeder longer.

If you work away from home or have limited patience or heirloom rugs, consider getting an adult. Breeders sometimes have retired adults available that would relish the chance to live as pampered pets, and rescue organizations have mostly adults. Adults may already be housetrained—but don't count on it! In fact, it may be more difficult to housetrain an adult who has been raised as a kennel dog.

Papers and Pedigrees

Most Dachshunds in the United States are registered with the American Kennel Club, and some are registered with the United Kennel Club. Canadian Dachshunds are registered with the Canadian Kennel Club, and Mexican ones with the Mexican Kennel Club. A bevy of other small registration bodies exist in North America, but most have minimal requirements, rendering registration with them meaningless. Registration with any kennel club is not an endorsement of quality. It simply certifies the dog is of pure Dachshund breeding, and relies a great deal on the honesty of the breeders submitting information.

Responsible breeders may sell companion-quality Dachshunds with Limited Registrations, which means

"Pick me! Pick me!"

that any offspring from those dogs could not be registered. Breeders do this to discourage breeding nonbreeding-quality dogs. The AKC also offers Indefinite Listing Privilege (ILP) registration to spayed or neutered dogs that are obviously Dachshunds but that do not have the paperwork to prove it. Dogs with Limited Registration or ILP numbers can compete in all AKC competitions except conformation.

Rescue Me!

The Dachshund's popularity, combined with the tendency of people to impulse buy and to underestimate the work involved in caring

How can you resist?

for any dog, has created an over-abundance of Dachshunds in need of new families. Some are advertised in the newspaper, some are forfeited to animal shelters, and some are fostered by Dachshund rescue organizations. Dachshunds end up in rescue for a number of reasons having nothing to do with them: a death, a divorce, a new baby in the family, or the family moving elsewhere. Some end up homeless because their family simply tired of them or became irritated at their barking, digging, house soiling, or other behaviors. A few are there because

of health or temperament problems. They have one thing in common: they are filled with love but have no one to give it to. They make us realize how special every Dachshund is.

Dachshund rescue groups are located throughout the country; a list can be found on page 158. Inviting a homeless Dachshund into your life is one of the most fulfilling ways you can find your special Dachshund.

As you open your heart to a Dachshund, you're taking the first steps in the adventure of a lifetime. Take steps now to have a safe trip and enjoy the journey.

Chapter Four
Raising Havoc

Welcome to the wonder months—your puppy's transition from life as one of a canine litter to life as one of a human family. These are some of the most important months for shaping your puppy's future. He'll need your help to be the best dog he can be.

Playing It Safe

Some people say preparing for a Dachshund puppy is like preparing for a baby, but those people underestimate the Dachshund. No human baby can gut a sofa, squeeze into ductwork, gnaw through a chair leg, eat his own body weight in garbage, or dance just out of your reach around the yard. Dachshund puppies are explorers. They will investigate parts of your house you haven't cleaned in years, be intimately acquainted with the undersides of your furniture, and lured by the treasures of your trash. You need to see the house from the Dachshund point of view to prevent carnage before it happens. When Dachshunds explore with their teeth, as they naturally do, it's not their fault

your belongings are ruined. You're the one who should have known better. Harsh corrections are no more effective than a tap on the nose along with a firm *"No,"* and removal of the item.

Puppies can damage not only your home but also themselves. They gnaw through electrical cords, lick electrical outlets, and tug on electrical cords until they pull over lamps. They can be crushed in slamming doors or caught in swinging doors, run into invisible glass doors, break through screen doors, or escape from open doors. They can fall down stairs or jump off high furniture. Fence off any danger areas, and consider making ramps leading to favorite perching places. These can be elaborate ramps with rails, or simply a stack of foam cushions. Otherwise teach your Dachshund to stay until you lift him down.

Dangers also abound within the yard. Check for poisonous plants, bushes with sharp, broken branches at Dachshund eye level, and trees with dead branches or heavy fruits or pine cones in danger of falling. If you have a pool, teach your Dachshund where the steps are and have him

Household Dangers
- Drugs
- Chocolate
- Rodent, snail, and insect poisons
- Antifreeze
- Household cleaners
- Toilet fresheners
- Nuts, bolts, or pennies
- Pins, needles, and thread
- Chicken bones or any bone that can be swallowed
- Sponges
- String, stockings, or any long item that can be swallowed

practice finding them in case he should ever fall in. Tiny puppies are at the mercy of predatory wildlife. Don't leave your puppy outside in an uncovered or unsecured area where coyotes, mountain lions, or large birds can be tempted.

The Dachshund Welcome Wagon

You can go wild buying Dachshund supplies. Here are some to consider:
- Food and water bowls: stainless steel bowls are the best, followed by ceramic. Plastic can cause allergic reactions in some dogs.
- Food: Start with what the breeder has been feeding and gradually change to your own brand.
- Collar: a cat collar may be best.
- Lightweight leash: a cat leash or an adjustable show lead works well.

- Lightweight retractable leash: more freedom without danger.
- Toys: latex squeakies, fleece-type toys, ball, stuffed animals, stuffed socks (especially stuffed with crackly sounding paper), or empty plastic soda jugs. Make sure no squeakers or plastic parts can be pulled off and swallowed.
- Chewbones: the equivalent of a baby's teething ring.
- Antichew sprays: the unpleasant taste dissuades pups from chewing.
- Crate: it should be large enough for an adult to stand up in.
- Exercise pen: a handy indoor yard.
- Baby gates: avoid accordion-style gates, which can close around a dog's neck.
- Nail clippers: guillotine-type clippers are easier to use.
- Dog shampoo (see page 50).
- First aid kit (see page 133).
- Poop scoop: two-piece rake-type scoop is best for grass.
- Dog coat or sweater: smaller dogs have greater heat loss because they have greater surface area compared to volume than large dogs do.

Identification. A well-fitting collar or harness with tags can help reunite you with a lost dog. A more permanent means of identification is a tattoo on your dog's inner thigh with your social security number or his AKC number. He can also have a tiny microchip implanted by means of a simple injection. Animal shelters have scanners that read the information from the chip. Information for both tattoos and microchips is stored in a central registry.

Planning the next escapade?

A safe haven. Dachshunds need to be not just in the house but also in the thick of things. They won't be happy banished to the garage or laundry room. Actually, they won't be happy until they've taken over your home and claimed it as their own. Your job is to come up with a compromise. Your Dachshund needs limits at first, for his safety as well as your home's. Use baby gates to shut off areas that are not for Dachshund occupancy. Use exercise pens to limit your dog to a small area inside when you can't watch him carefully. And use a cage (crate) when he needs to be confined to bed.

A crate is not a babysitter, a punishment, or a storage box for your dog. A Dachshund is an intelligent, active dog that needs stimulation. Incorrect use of the crate can lead to as many behavior problems as correct use can prevent. Used correctly, the crate can be an important asset. Place it in a quiet place not too far from family activities. Place a snuggly bed or blanket inside. Place him in the crate when he begins to fall asleep so he will become accustomed to using it as his bed. Your pup should ride in a crate in the car as a safety measure. If he enjoys going places, that's a good way to introduce him to the crate.

X-pen. X-pens (exercise pens) are transportable folding wire playpens for dogs, typically about 4 by 4 feet wide. They allow room for the pup to relieve himself on paper or in a litter-box in one corner, sleep on a soft bed in the other, and frolic with his toys all over! The X-pen provides a safe time-out area when you just

Puppies explore with their teeth, and sometimes stomach. Make sure your puppy doesn't explore poisonous plants.

need some quiet time for yourself or a safe holding area when you must be gone for a long time.

Fence. A fenced outside area leading from the back door is a big help in

Every penny you spend on toys will save you a dollar on shoes and home furnishings (miniature 10-week-old puppy).

raising and housetraining a dog. Make sure your fence is absolutely Dachshund-proof from the outset. Dachshunds were made for digging and squeezing; once they experience the thrill of victory over your fence, they learn to look even harder for vulnerable spots. For your dog's safety and your own peace of mind, get a fence you never have to worry about.

Invisible fences are not advisable for Dachshunds. The collar they must wear is too heavy, the shock they receive from crossing the boundary too intense, and the protection a real fence affords them against marauding dogs and dognappers is absent. Besides, many Dachshunds will grit their teeth and run through regardless of the shock.

Saving the Carpets

A pup running amuck in your home will shortly muck up your home with random deposits squirting from every orifice. That's why the number one rule of housetraining is to confine your dog. The best way to do this is to use a crate. Dogs naturally avoid soiling their sleeping spot and will avoid soiling their crate as long as it's not so big they can soil one end and sleep in the other, and as long as they have a choice. But pups can't hold themselves for long. A rule of thumb is that a pup can't hold itself any longer than the number of hours equivalent to how many months old it is; that is, a 3-month-old pup can hold itself for 3 hours.

Dogs prefer to return to the same toilet areas, which is why it's important for you to establish the desired areas quickly. As soon as your pup awakens, or after eating or heavy playing, take him to the toilet area and heap on the praise following his wonderful deed. Pups with access to doggy doors are particularly good at getting outside in time, but they still profit from your company and praise.

Accidents happen. Rubbing the dog's nose in his mess doesn't teach him anything except that every once in a while you go crazy and turn mean for no apparent reason.

Teach your Dachshund how to get out of a pool should he fall in.

Hello World!

Your Dachshund will need to meet his new world, including the people, places, and playmates he'll encounter as an adult. Although young puppies are relatively fearless, they become progressively more suspicious of novel experiences as they age. Puppies exposed to new things at an early age have a better chance of becoming confident adults.

Exposing doesn't mean overwhelming. Bad experiences are worse than no experiences at all. Good experiences should include treats, fun, and low stress exposure. Besides exposing your pup to men, women, children, dogs, cats, stairs, traffic, noises, car rides, swimming, grooming, and crate time, be sure to expose him to alone time. Dogs are social animals and don't like to be alone, but all dogs must learn to tolerate occasional

solitude. Start when your puppy is already tired, and casually leave him for just a little while. Giving him a novel interactive toy or chewy that is only available during these times can help ease the boredom.

Children

Puppies are child magnets, so you have to make sure your Dachshund isn't overwhelmed by a crowd of children all trying to pet him at once. Because a Dachshund is too easy to drop or step on, children should be seated on the floor when playing with one. They must be taught that Dachshunds can't be dropped, dangled, encouraged to jump off furniture, stepped on, fallen upon, or yanked off the ground in an overly vigorous game of tug o' war. Responsible, experienced children will learn to be careful enough so that they may play traditional dog games

outside, but for now, your puppy must be sheltered from accidents and overzealous handling.

Some older Dachshunds are wary of children, either because they don't understand them or because they've had bad experiences with them. Introduce adult Dachshunds and children carefully, encouraging the child to offer the dog a treat.

Any dog must be carefully supervised around babies. Introduce the dog to the baby gradually, rewarding him for being calm and well mannered. Always make a fuss over the dog when the baby is present. Never shuttle him out of the room because the baby is coming in. You want the dog to associate the baby with good times, not to be resentful.

Dogs and Other Animals

Dachshunds tend to be clannish, forming close friendships with canine housemates but often challenging

Meeting other dogs is an important part of growing up.

strange dogs. Many Dachshunds are true to their hunting heritage and won't hesitate to chase a wild animal or even a tame one they imagine could be wild. Introduce other family pets carefully. If you have a cat, feed them together, and don't allow either one to run after or from the other. Make sure other, more entertaining things are available to distract your dog. Once they get used to one another, Dachshunds and cats can become close friends.

Dachshund Pediatrics

Like all youngsters, Dachshund puppies need your help to grow up healthy. Your veterinarian can guide you through the best preventive health care regime for your dog, including vaccinations, deworming, and possibly neutering or spaying.

Vaccinations

Before your puppy ventures out into a world full of viruses and disease, he will need to be properly vaccinated. Puppies receive their dam's immunity from colostrum, the special type of milk she produces in the first days of the pups' lives. This passive immunity will wear off after several weeks, but there's no way to know exactly when. If it wears off, your pup will be vulnerable; but if vaccinations are given before it wears off, they won't be effective, and your pup will be equally vulnerable. Thus, a series of vaccinations are given in order to catch the immune system at the earliest time the vaccinations will take effect.

Nothing is gained by vaccinating too much, or by vaccinating an already ill dog. Vaccinations occasionally cause adverse reactions, prompting some owners of little dogs to advocate using smaller doses. However, veterinary consensus is that all dogs require the same vaccine dose regardless of size. This is because stimulation of the body's immune system doesn't depend on the concentration of the vaccine in the body but rather on the absolute amount of vaccine—just as it takes the same level of a virus to infect both large and small dogs.

Vaccinations are divided into core vaccines, which are advisable for all

Make sure your puppy is properly vaccinated before venturing out in public.

dogs, and noncore vaccines, which are advisable for only some dogs. Core vaccines are those for rabies, distemper, parvovirus, and hepatitis (using the CAV-2 vaccine). Noncore vaccines include those for leptospirosis, corona virus, tracheobronchitis, Lyme disease, and giardia. Your veterinarian can advise you if your dog's life-style and environment put him at risk for these diseases.

Veterinary organizations have recently revised their vaccination protocols to include fewer booster shots. One such protocol suggests giving a three-shot series for puppies, each shot containing distemper (or measles for the first series), parvovirus, adenovirus 2 (CAV-2), parainfluenza (CPIV), and distemper, with one rabies vaccination at 16 weeks. Following this a booster is given one year later, with subsequent boosters every 3 years. Various protocols are still being evaluated, so your veterinarian may advocate a different one than this; let your veterinarian know you're interested in hearing his opinion of the pros and cons of various regimes.

Deworming

Internal parasites can be devastating for a tiny puppy. The number one prevention for most worms is daily removal of feces from the yard. Some heartworm preventives also prevent most types of intestinal worms (but not tapeworms). Over-the-counter dewormers are neither as effective nor safe as those available from your veterinarian. A laboratory stool check can determine the type of parasite your dog may have and direct the veterinarian to the best treatment for it. For these reasons your Dachshund should be dewormed only under the supervision of your veterinarian.

Your pup should have been checked and dewormed if needed before coming home with you, but you should recheck. Even puppies from the most fastidious breeders can get worms because some types of larval worms can lie dormant and safe from deworming in the dam long before she ever becomes pregnant, waiting for hormonal changes caused by her pregnancy to become active and infect her puppies. Your dog may also pick up worms from areas where lots of dogs congregate.

The most common intestinal parasites are ascarids, hookworms, whip-worms, tapeworms, and protozoa such as coccidian and giardia. Diarrhea, weight loss, and other signs can signal the presence of any of these parasites. The best way to detect them is with a fecal check.

Tapeworms are a common parasite of dogs of all ages. They look like moving white flat worms when fresh, or like rice grains (usually around the dog's anus) when dried out. Although they are one of the least debilitating of all the worms, their segments can produce anal itching. Because tapeworms are in the cestode family, they are not affected by the same kinds of dewormers and preventives as the other common worms, which are in the nematode family. The best preventive is diligently to rid your dog of fleas because fleas transmit the most common tapeworm *(Dipylidium)* to dogs. Your veterinarian can provide medication for ridding your dog of tapeworms once they are present.

Heartworm Prevention

Heartworms are killers. Wherever mosquitoes are present, dogs should be on heartworm prevention. Your pup should start taking the preventive at an early age; the exact time will depend on his exposure to mosquitoes. Monthly preventives don't stay in the dog's system for a month, but instead act on a particular stage in the heartworm's development. Giving the drug each month prevents any heartworms from ever maturing. The most common way of checking for heartworms is to check the blood for circulating microfilarae (immature heartworms), but this method may miss adult heartworms in as many as 20 percent of all tested dogs. More accurate is an "occult" heartworm test, which detects antigens to heartworms in the blood. With either test, heartworms will not be detectable until nearly 7 months after infection. While treatable in their early stages, it is expensive and not without risk.

Spaying and Neutering

You will probably find life easier if your Dachshund is spayed or neutered. If you think you'd like to breed a litter, consider first all the reasons not to breed (page 137). An intact (unspayed) female will come into estrus, or season, usually around 8 months of age. This will last for about 3 weeks, during which she will have a bloody discharge that can stain your furnishings. For part of that time she will be enticing and receptive to males, so you must keep her isolated. Intact (unneutered) males seldom suffer in silence and can make life miserable for anyone within earshot. A month or two after her season a female will often have a false pregnancy, which can be so convincing you will wonder where you slipped up. She may have milk and even adopt a toy as though it were a puppy.

Besides your mental health, canine health reasons exist for spaying and neutering. Intact females are at increased risk of developing pyometra, a potentially fatal infection of the uterus, and breast cancer. Spaying before her first season dras-tically reduces the chance of breast cancer in later life. Intact male dogs are more likely to roam or fight. They are also more likely to develop testicular cancer. The major drawbacks are that some neutered or spayed dogs gain weight and some spayed females can develop urinary incontinence. Talk to your veterinarian about all the pros and cons.

Baby Food

Feeding any puppy is important; feeding a small puppy is critical. Your Dachshund should eat a high-quality puppy food, and should eat many times a day. Poor feeding practices can lead not only to poor nutrition, poor growth, and poor health but also to a potentially fatal condition called hypoglycemia.

Hypoglycemia

Hypoglycemia is a disorder of the central nervous system caused by low blood sugar. It occurs most often in small, young, stressed or active dogs, such as miniature Dachshund puppies. These dogs aren't able to store enough readily available glucose, so once the available glycogen (the form in which the body stores glucose) is depleted the body begins to break down energy stored in fat. Small puppies have very little subcutaneous fat, however, so that energy is soon depleted. When that happens, the brain, which depends on glucose-derived energy to function, ceases to function properly. Signs such as sleepiness, weakness, and loss of appetite and coordination may

Protect your Dachshund puppy from chilling.

appear suddenly. Left untreated, the condition can worsen until the dog has seizures, loses consciousness, and dies.

Meals should be fairly high in protein, fat, and complex carbohydrates. Complex carbohydrates slow the breakdown of carbohydrates into sugars, which should lead to more efficient utilization. Avoid semimoist foods because of their high sugar content, as well as other simple sugars such as syrup unless your dog is already showing signs of hypoglycemia.

If you suspect your dog is having a hypoglycemic episode, immediately feed him a high-sugar-content food such as Karo syrup. (If he is unconscious, smear it on his gums—do not put it down his throat!) You should see improvement within 2 minutes; use this time to alert your veterinarian that you are bringing him in immediately for treatment, possibly with intravenous glucose. Once the dog is stronger and able to swallow, it's important to immediately give him a small, high-protein meal, such as beef or chicken baby food.

Hypoglycemia is mostly a problem of puppies (it may be related to immaturity of liver cells), and most dogs will outgrow it by the time they reach about 7 months of age.

Puppy Grooming

Now is the time to accustom your Dachshund to the pleasures of grooming. Use a soft brush and gently stroke him with it. Handle his feet and then eventually use the nail clippers to just nip the smallest bit off the ends of his toenails. Rub your finger along his teeth, then graduate to a soft dog toothbrush. Give lots of treats as you go along!

Chapter Five
Dachshund Diets

If you leave the choice of diet to your Dachshund, she'll make the choice easy: whatever's on your plate. But despite what she thinks, Dachshunds aren't little people in fur coats, and what's good for people, isn't necessarily good for dogs. The diet you choose for your Dachshund is one of the most important but confusing decisions you'll make.

The Nature of Nutrition

Your Dachshund may consider herself a card-carrying carnivore, but the secret truth is, she's really an omnivore. Dachshunds do not live by meat alone. Her nutritional needs are best met by a diet rich in meat that also includes vegetable matter. A good rule of thumb is that three or four of the first six ingredients of a dog food should be animal derived. Animal ingredients are more appealing to dogs and more highly digestible than plant-based ingredients. More highly digestible foods generally mean less stool volume and fewer gas problems.

Different diets provide different amounts of nutrients. Nutrients are divided into water, vitamins, minerals, protein, fat, and carbohydrates.

Water is vital to life. It dissolves and transports other substances, takes part in chemical reactions, assists in regulating body temperature, helps lubricate joints, and aids in gas exchange when breathing. Water deprivation can lead to death within days, and dehydration can cause or complicate many health problems.

Vitamins are organic components essential in tiny amounts for normal life function. Dogs require three fat-soluble vitamins (A, D, and E) and eight water-soluble vitamins (B_1, B_2, B_{12}, niacin, pyridoxine, pantothenic acid, folic acid, and choline). Vitamins have diverse but important roles in many body functions. Most pet foods have added vitamins to achieve the optimal amounts required.

Minerals are inorganic components in foods. They help build body organs and tissue, are components of many body fluids, and are part of enzyme and hormone systems. For example, calcium, phosphorus, and

"Feed me!"

magnesium are important components of bones and teeth. Sodium, potassium, and chloride are important parts of blood, cerebrospinal fluid, and gastric juice. Depending on the mineral, deficiencies can cause anemia, poor growth, poor or strange appetite, fractures, convulsions, vomiting, weakness, heart problems, and many other disorders. Excesses can cause just as many problems.

Proteins consist of amino acids. They provide the principal structure of the body's tissues and organs, the components needed for muscles to contract, cartilage to stretch, and hair to grow. They provide important blood components such as hemoglobin, and also function as enzymes, hormones, and antibodies. Dogs require ten essential amino acids that

can only be provided by eating proteins containing them. Not all proteins contain the same amino acids, and not all proteins are equally digestible. This means that proteins from different sources may supply different nutrition. Eggs, followed by meat-derived proteins, are higher quality and more highly digestible than plant-derived proteins. Most pet foods contain a variety of protein sources in order to provide a complement of amino acids. Others contain specific amino acids added to fortify the foods when the main protein source may be lacking that component.

Fats are technically lipids, which refer to both fats and oils. They supply energy and essential fatty acids and aid in the absorption of fat-soluble vitamins. Dogs deficient in fatty acids may have delayed wound healing, scaly skin, a dry coat, and other skin problems. They may also lose weight, both because low-fat foods are less tasty and because they provide fewer calories. Too much fat, however, can cause obesity and appetite reduction, creating a deficiency in other nutrients.

Carbohydrates provide energy in the form of glucose, which the brain and red blood cells require for energy. Glucose can also be derived from fats and proteins if carbohydrate intake is inadequate, but this method is less efficient. Most commercial foods contain more carbohydrates than necessary, partly because they are an inexpensive source of energy. Carbohydrates derived from rice are best utilized, those from potato and

Your Dachshund may imagine itself a wild dog living off the land, but it depends on you to fill its bowl with tasty nutritious food, whether commercial or home-prepared.

corn far less so, and wheat, oat, and beans even less again.

Fiber refers to complex carbohydrates that differ from starches in that they can't be digested. They include ingredients such as beat pulp, rice bran, gums, and peanut hulls. Fiber normalizes the moisture of intestinal contents, which means it's helpful in treating both constipation and diarrhea. Fiber, especially slowly fermentable fibers such as peanut hulls or cellulose, are often used in weight-reducing diets both to make the dog feel full and to prevent digestibility of some of the other nutrients. Too much fiber can interfere with digestion of other nutrients and cause large stool volume.

A dog's optimal diet will change according to its age, energy requirements, and state of health. Prescription commercial diets and recipes for home-prepared diets are available for dogs with special needs. It is a tribute to the dog's general hardiness that most dogs survive eating some of the worst diets. But you want your Dachshund to do more than simply survive; you want her to thrive. You want her to have the best chance at a long healthy life, and you want her to enjoy her meals. Varying her diet can provide some insurance that she's getting proper nutrition by providing a wide range of ingredients. In fact, most dogs tend to prefer a novel food, but then tire of it within a few days. The problem is that many dogs develop diarrhea at abrupt changes in diet, so you must change foods gradually with most dogs.

Natural Versus Commercial

Wild canids evolved eating a diet consisting largely of raw meat plus the vegetable matter within their prey's stomach. The earliest domesticated dogs subsisted largely on human garbage as well as whatever they could catch or forage themselves. For many centuries domestic dogs ate mostly leftovers, scraps, and bread products. Only in recent decades have commercial foods been available. Some people think that commercial diets consisting of processed foods are so far removed from the dog's natural diet that they are creating unhealthy dogs. Others believe that commercial diets are healthier than trying to create a balanced diet on your own.

Commercial Foods

Critics of commercial foods contend they are highly processed, do not resemble a dog's natural diet, are not fresh, and may use ingredients unfit for human consumption. Proponents of commercial foods point out that these diets have been tested on generations of dogs and meticulously adjusted to provide optimal nutrition.

The Association of American Feed Control Officials (AAFCO) has outlined minimal nutritional requirements a food must meet. Better foods meet these through feeding trials, and this will be printed on the bag. Better premium commercial foods often use human-grade ingredients.

Commercial foods come in dry, canned, and semimoist varieties, as well as treats.

• Dry food (containing about 10 percent moisture) is the most popular, economical, and healthy—but least enticing—form of dog food. It can be especially difficult for dogs with tooth problems to eat large kibble. Dry food loses nutrients as it sits, and the fat content can become rancid, so you should only buy small bags for your Dachshund.

• Canned food has a high moisture content (about 75 percent), which helps to make it tasty, but it is also comparatively expensive, since you're in essence buying water.

• Moist foods (with about 30 percent moisture) contain high levels of sugar used as preservatives. Although they are tasty and convenient, they are not an optimal nutritional choice as a regular diet and especially not suggested as a regular meal in any dog prone to hypoglycemia (see page 39).

• Treats are usually dry or moist. They don't have to meet AAFCO requirements for a nutritionally balanced diet because they are not intended to make up an entire diet.

To compare the nutrients of wet, moist, and dry foods, you must first equate them for moisture content. The most accurate way to do this is to get the food's dry matter content by subtracting the percentage of water listed. For example, a canned food with 75 percent water would have 25 percent dry matter. Then divide the percentage of each nutrient by the

Nothing's as much fun as a wiener dog picnic—especially when nobody's watching!

food's total dry matter percentage. To figure the dry matter percentage of protein in a canned food that was 75 percent water and 10% protein, divide 10 percent by 25 percent. This would show you that the canned food contained 40 percent protein on a dry matter basis.

If you're not mathematically inclined, you can fudge by figuring approximate values. Do this by adding 10% to each nutrient for dry foods or multiplying each nutrient by 4 for moist foods, and then comparing these values to the listed canned food label values.

Raw Food

If wolves eat whole raw animal carcasses, then why shouldn't dogs? That's the idea behind feeding raw food diets, and it does make intuitive sense. But too many people who feed raw diets don't do it that way; after all, most people prefer to feed parts of animals, discarding the head, fur, feet, organs, and stomach contents. Many people oversimplify these diets, perhaps feeding an exclusive diet of chicken wings, which is neither natural nor balanced. They too often follow secondhand advice without basing their diets on tested recipes.

Controlled studies on the safety and efficacy of raw diets have yet to be published. The few controlled studies of the nutritional value of commonly used raw diets have shown most are lacking in important nutrients. Critics worry that raw foods from processing plants may pose the threat of salmonella and *E. coli*. Although, compared to people, dogs are more resistant to illness from these bacteria, they are not immune. If raw food is fed, it should be fresh, locally processed, ground thoroughly, and prepared following a legitimate recipe.

"This scale must be wrong..."

study nutrition and have your diet tested by a pet food nutrition tester, then it may be possible for you to devise a diet actually superior to a commercial one. However, very few owners can do this.

The third choice is a raw diet. This is only a good choice if you can obtain fresh clean meat and can follow a proven diet. Again, very few owners can do this.

Home-Prepared Food

Home-prepared, cooked diets from recipes developed by canine nutritionists may provide the safest and best compromise between commercial and raw diets. The downside is that they are more labor intensive than either. Do not try to devise such a recipe yourself; canine nutrition is not the same as human nutrition, and the chance of you cooking up a balanced diet is slim.

Which Is Best?

For most Dachshund owners, a high-quality "premium" commercial food is the best bet. Such foods are found in pet supermarkets and cost slightly more than typical grocery store dog foods. You can add a high-quality canned food for extra flavor. It will not hurt to feed your Dachshund occasional table scraps and treats, but they should not make up a large part of the diet.

The second best choice is cooking a home-prepared diet. If you

Feeding Time!

Your Dachshund has several highlights of his day: waking you up, going for a walk, welcoming you home, and, at the top of the list, eating. Traditional dog dogma contends that adult dogs should only be fed once a day, but your Dachshund begs to differ. Although she may claim Dachshunds should eat ten times a day, a more reasonable schedule gives your adult Dachshund a small meal in the morning and a large meal in the evening, or vice versa.

Very young puppies should be fed at least four times a day, on a regular schedule. Feed them as much as they care to eat in about 15 minutes. From the age of 3 to 6 months, pups should be fed three to four times daily, and two to three times daily until they are about a year old. After that, they should eat twice daily. If you choose to feed more often, make sure to adjust meal size so that you are not feeding your dog too much. If your schedule is unpredictable, you may wish to leave dry food available at all times. Many Dachshunds will overeat when given this choice, however. Another disadvantage is that you won't realize as quickly if your dog is off her feed, and so you may miss an early sign of illness.

Weight Problems

Perhaps the biggest and most common feeding problem is allowing your Dachshund to get fat. The Dachshund is a naturally slender dog. If she becomes overweight the additional stress on her back can aggravate spinal problems. Obesity also predisposes dogs to joint injuries and heart problems.

You can't feed your dog according to a product's recommended amounts, or even according to what your other Dachshund eats. Like people, dogs are individuals each with a different metabolism, so each dog's diet must be adjusted accordingly.

In proper weight, your Dachshund should have a trim outline with a slightly smaller waist than chest. The ribs should be easily felt through a layer of muscle, but they should not feel like a washboard. There should be no roll of fat over the withers or rump, but neither the backbone nor the hipbones should be prominent.

Your dog should be checked for health problems before embarking on any serious weight reduction effort. Heart disease and some endocrine disorders, such as hypothyroidism or

Deciphering the Ingredient List
• *Meat:* mammal flesh including muscle, skin, heart, esophagus, and tongue.
• *Meat by-products:* cleaned mammal organs including kidneys, stomach, intestines, brain, spleen, lungs, and liver, plus blood, bone, and fatty tissue products, not including blood.
• *Poultry by-products:* cleaned poultry organs, plus feet and heads.
• *Poultry by-products meal:* product rendered from processed poultry by-products.
• *Fish meal:* dried ground fish.
• *Beef tallow:* fat.
• *Soybean meal:* by-product of soybean oil.
• *Corn meal:* ground entire corn kernels.
• *Corn gluten meal:* dried residue after the removal of bran, germ, and starch from corn.
• *Brewer's rice:* fragmented rice kernels separated from milled rice.
• *Cereal food fines:* small particles of human breakfast cereals.
• *Beet pulp:* dried residue from sugar beets, added for fiber.
• *Peanut hulls:* ground peanut shells, added for fiber.
• *BRA, BHT, ethoxyquin, sodium nitrate, tocopherols (vitamins C and E):* preservatives. Of these, the tocopherols are generally considered to present the fewest health risks, but they also have the shortest shelf life.

Cushing's disease, or the early stages of diabetes, can cause the appearance of obesity and should be ruled out or treated. A dog in which only the stomach is enlarged is especially suspect and should be examined by a veterinarian.

If your veterinarian determines that you simply have a fat Dachshund, it's time for tough love. Feed smaller portions and a lower calorie food. Commercially available diet foods supply about 15 percent fewer calories. Research indicates that protein levels should remain moderate to high in reducing diets in order to avoid the loss of muscle tissue. Tasty low-calorie home-prepared diets are available; ask your veterinarian. Substitute low-calorie snack alternatives such as rice cakes or carrots. Resist those pleading eyes—if you can! You may have better luck keeping her out of the room when you eat or prepare food. Schedule a walk immediately following your dinner to get your dog's mind off your leftovers—it will be good for both of you.

Thin Dachshunds are less common. A Dachshund that loses weight rapidly or steadily for no apparent reason should have a veterinary exam because many diseases can cause weight and appetite loss. Underweight dogs may gain weight with puppy food; add milk, bouillon, ground beef, chicken fat, or canned food and heat slightly to increase aroma and palatability. Milk will cause many dogs to have diarrhea, so try only a little bit at first. A sick or recuperating dog may have to be coaxed into eating. Both cat food and meat baby food are relished by dogs and may entice a dog without an appetite to eat. Try cooking chicken breasts or other meat, but ask your veterinarian first.

Chapter Six

The Dapper Dachshund

Dachshunds are dirt dogs. They are in their element when they're getting down and dirty, and if some of that element happens to stick to them so much the better. And if they can transfer an element of the great outdoors inside with them, then life is indeed good. At least that's what they think.

People are funny, though. They like to run their hands through a clean coat and snuggle with a fresh-smelling dog. And they like their dogs to look at least somewhat like they are supposed to look. Your idea and your Dachshund's idea of good grooming may differ, but you're the one holding the brushes.

Basic Coat Care

It's not that difficult to keep your Dachshund well-groomed. Whether you have a Smooth, Longhaired, or Wirehaired Dachshund, he will look and feel better if his coat is clean. Grooming is not only important for the sake of beauty, but it also can prevent serious health problems. Just as with people, good grooming involves more than an occasional brushing of the hair. Keeping the nails, teeth, eyes, and ears well groomed is just as, if not more, important.

Casual grooming can be done with your dog seated beside you on a blanket, but if you're serious about your results a grooming table is essential. Most come with a grooming arm from which hangs an adjustable loop (called a grooming noose) to hold the dog still while grooming, freeing up both of your hands. You must never step away from the table when your dog is on it, lest he jump off and either hurt himself or hang by the noose.

Shedding

All Dachshunds shed. Shedding is controlled by light levels, so dogs kept indoors tend to shed somewhat all year long, with a heavy spring shed. A daily vigorous brushing during shedding season, using a stiff bristle brush, rubber curry brush, or slicker brush, is the best way to control loose hair. More hairs will shed after bathing, and they are especially easy to dislodge when the hair is almost, but not quite, dry. Wire coats tend to hang in there a little longer

Good grooming shows.

and will need help in the form of plucking or stripping to dislodge dead hair.

Bathing and Drying

Most dirt can be brushed out of healthy Dachshund hair, and unless your dog has found something delightful to dogs but disgusting to people to roll in, you shouldn't have to bathe him often. An occasional bath will make his hair softer and better smelling. Of course, you don't want your Wirehaired Dachshund to have soft wire hair before a show, so bathing a Wirehaired should be done a week or so before show time. Other varieties are best done just before showing or, if dandruff is a problem, a couple of days before a show.

Shampoo Selection

If your dog has healthy skin and coat and you just want a simple bath, using a human shampoo or even a liquid dish washing detergent will work fine. Dog shampoos give best results because they are formulated for the dog's skin pH of 7.5 as opposed to the human skin pH of 5.5. Texturizing and terrier coat shampoos are available that will help wire coats remain harsh.

Shampoos are available from your veterinarian and are effective for various skin problems. Oatmeal-based antipruritics can help sooth itchy skin, moisturizing shampoos can help with dry skin, antiseborrheic shampoos can help with excessive greasy scaling and dandruff, and antimicrobials can help damaged skin. No dog owner should be without one of the dog shampoos that requires no water or rinsing. These are wonderful for puppies, spot-baths, and emergencies.

Bathing

Place a nonskid mat in the bottom of your tub or sink. A handheld sprayer is essential for indoor bathing. Remember to use water that you would be comfortable using for a shower. Warm water tends to open the hair follicles and helps to loosen dead hair. Keep one hand under the spray so you can monitor the water temperature.

Wet the dog, leaving the head for last. Be sure the water soaks down to the skin. Mix the shampoo with water first. Use a big sponge to

At some point in the early days of dog shows it became the fad to snip off the whiskers, or vibrissae, on a dog's head as part of show grooming. This has slowly become less fashionable, and more people now leave these important sensory organs on their dogs both at home and in the ring. Field trial competitors report that dogs with missing vibrissae are more prone to facial cuts.

apply it and then use your hands to work up a moderate lather. Rinsing is a crucial step; shampoo remaining in the coat can cause dryness and itchiness. Begin rinsing from the front and top of the dog and work backwards and rearwards. To keep your dog from shaking, keep one hand clenched around the base of one ear. You can use a small amount of crème rinse for Smooths and Longhaireds but not Wirehaireds.

Drying

Don't let your dog outside on a chilly day when still wet from a bath. You have removed the oils from the coat and saturated him down to the skin. Towel drying will help dislodge any remaining dead hairs. You can hasten drying with a blow dryer, but take care not to burn your dog. Never place a dog in an enclosed crate with the blow dryer aimed at him. Many dogs have died this way from overheating. Blow drying long hair will tend to make it puffier than is

ideal for the show ring. To avoid this blow the hair in the direction of growth. If the hair is dry and fly away, instead of blow drying place a towel over the dog's back and pin it under his neck and belly so the towel absorbs the water.

Grooming the Smooth Coat

The Smooth coat is remarkably care-free. It should be brushed weekly with a soft natural bristle brush or hound glove, and bathed occasionally. If you're showing, you can carefully snip off any scraggly hairs around the breastbone, the sides of the neck, and beneath the tail, but undergroomed is preferable to overgroomed. Finish with a slight mist of grooming spray and burnish with a soft cloth.

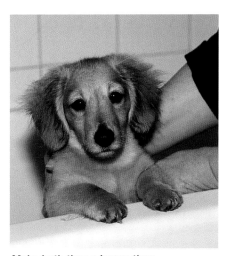

Make bath time a happy time.

Grooming the Long Coat

The Longhaired Dachshund requires brushing every few days to keep the coat tangle-free. Always mist the coat with water from a spritzing bottle before brushing. This will cut down on static electricity and resulting tangles and fly-away hair; it will also lessen hair breakage. Use a pin brush or comb. If you find a mat, try to break it apart lengthwise, combing bits of hair out of the mat until it goes away. Cutting the mat out will leave the coat looking ragged, and the hair is more likely to mat again when growing back. Always make sure no mats or tangles are in the coat before bathing, since the water tends to make them worse.

Comb long hair in its direction of growth.

Your Dachshund will probably need some slight trimming to look his best. However, the Dachshund is a natural breed that should never be sculpted into a perfect silhouette. The coat should not be excessively long; if your dog has extremely long feathering, you may wish to shorten it so that leaves and sticks are less likely to get caught in it—but it's so pretty you won't want to do too much. If you trim before (rather than after) bathing you can better achieve a natural look.

If you are grooming for the show ring, you will need to do some additional thinning or trimming. Sometimes the hair grows too thick in some areas, particularly over the withers, giving the illusion of a lumpy topline. In fact the entire neck area may be covered in thick hair that causes the neck to look short and fat. You want the coat to be short on the underside of the neck, gradually blossoming into a full apron just above the breastbone. You can carefully use a stripping knife or thinning shears to remove some of the excess coat, but on some dogs the remaining hair will be a lighter color—this is not something to try the night before the show! This is a particular problem with reds and chocolates. It's best to do most thinning about 6 weeks before the show so the hair will be the same color at show time.

Use a stripping comb or shears to remove fluffy hair under the ear to allow the ear to lie closer to the head. The ears may have excess hair

How to Use Dachshund Grooming Tools

A stripping comb (or knife) is a serrated tool in which a sharp cutting surface is between the small teeth. They come in various blade sizes, with the coarser ones better for heavy stripping and the finer ones more suitable for finishing touches. When combed through the dog's fur in the direction of growth, it removes any dead hair and quite a bit of the live hair. Because it tends to cut hair, it can give a rough appearance, especially if used too enthusiastically. Hold the skin taut in the area you are combing; otherwise the comb tends to catch the skin. To use the stripping comb with wire hair, hold a small amount of hair between the tool and your thumb, and quickly jerk the comb directly backward in the direction of hair growth. If you add a slight twisting motion, the comb will cut the hairs, which can lead to patches of overly short coat. You should try to avoid twisting the comb unless you are really trying to cut hair. When using the stripping comb to give a final, neat appearance, comb it straight through the hair without any twisting motion.

A lava stripping stone is a very coarse pumice stone that can be brushed over the coat in the direction of growth to remove fine fuzzy hair. Overly vigorous use will scratch the skin.

Thinning shears are scissors with one edge having comblike teeth. It's often most effective to first backbrush hair you wish to thin. Then place the shears as close to the skin as possible. Most people err by cutting across the hair growth, but it's essential that you place the shears in line with the hair growth. For example, if you are thinning the hair over the withers, the shears should be in the same line as the dog's body, not lying across the withers. Take a snip or two, comb the hair down, judge the results, and repeat if needed.

Electric clippers can be used to cut a wire coat shorter, as long as you don't wish to show the dog. Cut wire hair tends to lack the correct harsh texture that a stripped coat retains. Cut in the direction of hair growth. The higher the blade number, the shorter the cut. A #10 blade will cut the hair very short, and is best used only on the head, ears, and under the neck. A #7, or especially a #5, leaves the hair longer and is a better choice for the body hair.

on the top where they join the skull. You can remove this, as well as any crazed hair sticking up rooster-fashion on the head, by plucking by hand or by using a lava stripping stone.

Comb along the back of the neck all the way to the tail with a stripping comb, removing overly thick hair and striving to create a seamless sleek and graceful line. Continue to comb partway down the sides, letting the hair become gradually longer so no abrupt line between short and long hair mars the look.

The tail is generally not trimmed, but allowed to grow naturally.

The hair behind the front and rear legs should be profuse, but not so much so that it appears bushy or sticks out to the sides. Do what you can to convince it to lie flat just behind the legs by spraying it with water and then blow drying it in position. If parts still stick out, use the thinning shears to remove the outer layers carefully.

Use small scissors to cut the scraggly hairs around each foot so that the foot has a clean-cut round appearance. Don't forget the hairs beneath the feet, which can become long and slippery and also tend to accumulate debris from your yard.

To strip the coat, grasp some hair between your thumb and the stripping tool and pull quickly in the direction of hair growth.

The hair should be cut to no longer than the level of the foot pads.

Don't do too perfect a job. Dachshunds should look like they just stepped out of the field rather than the beauty parlor. When in doubt, don't cut it out!

Grooming the Wire Coat

Grooming the Wirehaired Dachshund may seem initially daunting, but it's not difficult once you've done it a few times. Left ungroomed, Wirehaireds tend to grow into tumbleweeds, losing their dapper streamlined appearance. Start with a good brushing with a bristle brush a few times a week.

As the wire coat grows, it will eventually become dry and dead looking. Use a stripping comb to remove much of the coat. You can also pluck the coat, grasping a few longer hairs between the thumb and index finger and pulling abruptly. Whether stripping or plucking, be sure to pull the hair only in the direction it's growing.

If the hair doesn't come out easily with plucking or stripping, it may not be ready. Unless you have a show date looming, it's best to just wait another week or two. Some people are simply uncomfortable pulling out their dog's hair, despite the fact that when done at the correct time the dog seems oblivious to it.

Clipping the coat can also be considered if you have no plans to show your dog. Clipping doesn't remove the dead hairs, but simply cuts them, so they will still eventually shed. In addition, the coat will be somewhat duller and less richly colored and will feel softer because the undercoat will be exposed. If you choose to clip your dog, leave the coat fairly long by clipping in the direction of hair growth and using a blade, such as a #7, that doesn't cut closely. Although you won't achieve a proper wire coat, your Dachshund will still have a smart, clean appearance with a fraction of the effort. You can have a professional groomer clip him, but most grooming shops do not strip or pluck.

Deciding what to strip short and what to keep long isn't so difficult. The Wirehaired Dachshund should have a close fitting jacket over most of his body. Only on the muzzle and eyebrows is the hair appreciably long. Specifically, the hair should be short from the corner of the lip to the outer corner of the eye, with any longer hairs also removed from the area just under the eyes. The top of the skull should be short, with the eyebrows left long but tapering shorter toward the outside eye corner where they blend into the shorter cheek hair. The beard should get gradually fuller and longer as it approaches the end of the muzzle. Any longer hairs of the ears should be removed.

The hair of the neck and body should be stripped short, to about a half inch or a little longer, following

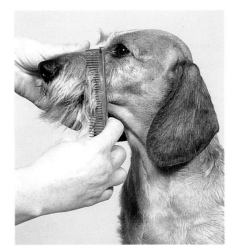
Comb wire facial furnishings forward.

the body contours and taking care to maintain smooth lines throughout. The hair on the legs can be longer than the body hair. Trim the feet as you would on a Longhaired Dachshund.

If you let your dog get overgrown, you may need to do a major stripping job. Because the coat will need time to look its best, this should be done about 2 months before an important show. The coat can then be plucked judiciously to maintain it at the optimal length.

Plucking

Test the coat to see if it is ready for plucking by grasping a few hairs and giving them a quick tug. If they don't pull out easily, then wait a week or two and try again.

Don't bathe your dog before plucking. Dirtier hair is easier to grasp. Grooming chalk is available to make the hair even less slippery. Use a pin or slicker brush to brush the hair in both directions to remove as much loose hair as possible and to help loosen the remaining hair. Apply the grooming chalk, then comb the hair backwards so that it stands off the body.

To pluck hair, hold the skin taut by pulling it with one hand. Use your index finger and thumb to grasp a few of the long hairs of the outer coat just above the shorter hairs of the undercoat (usually about an inch from the skin), and pull them sharply in the direction of hair growth.

Coat and Skin Problems

A healthy coat depends on healthy skin. Skin problems make up most of the "non-well" cases a veterinarian sees every day. Problems can result from parasites, allergies, bacteria,

A smooth coat in good condition shines.

fungus, endocrine disorders, and a long list of other possible causes.

Clean Dachshunds should not have a strong body odor. Doggy odor is not only offensive; it is unnatural. Check the mouth, ears, feet, anus, and genitals for infection. Impacted anal sacs can contribute to bad odor. Generalized bad odor can indicate a skin problem, such as seborrhea. Don't ignore bad odor, and don't make your dog take the blame for something you need to fix.

Dermatophytosis

Dermatophytosis, better known as ringworm, is one of the most common fungal disorders of dogs. Ringworm is contagious to other animals (including humans), so a dog with ringworm should be managed with this in mind. It can also be transmitted by direct contact with contaminated objects (such as combs) and, in some cases, from soil in which the ringworm fungi reside.

The most common areas of infection are the head and forelimbs. The fungi invade the outermost layers of the skin, along with the nails and hair, causing an expanding area of hair loss with crusting, redness, and scaling around the margins. Diagnosis is by several means, including examination under a special ultraviolet light, microscopic examination, and culture. Often the disease will go away by itself after a few months, but treatment with antifungal medications is suggested. The environment should be thoroughly cleaned, including bleaching and steam cleaning where possible.

Skin Allergies

Flea allergy dermatitis (FAD) is the most common of all skin problems. When even one flea bites a susceptible dog the flea's saliva causes an allergic reaction that results in intense itching, not only in the vicinity of the flea bite, but often all over the dog and especially on its rump, legs, and paws. The dog chews these areas and causes irritation leading to crusted bumps.

Besides FAD, dogs can have allergic reactions to pollens or other inhaled allergens. Whereas human inhalant allergies usually result in respiratory symptoms, canine inhalant allergies usually result in itchy skin. The condition typically first appears in young dogs and gets progressively worse. The main sites of itching seem to be the face, ears, feet, forelegs, armpits, and abdomen. The dog rubs and chews these areas, traumatizing the skin and leading to secondary bacterial infections. Because the feet are so often affected, many people erroneously assume the dog is allergic to grass or dew. Although such contact allergies do exist, they are far less common than flea, inhalant, or food allergies.

Allergens can be isolated with an intradermal skin test, in which small amounts of various allergen extracts are injected under the skin. The skin is then monitored for localized allergic reactions. Blood tests are also available and are less expensive, but they are not as comprehensive as skin testing. Either test should be performed by a veterinarian with training

The Longhaired Dachshund should retain its sleek lines.

in the field of allergic skin diseases, as the results can be difficult to interpret.

External Parasites

Parasites remain one of the most common causes of skin and coat problems in dogs. Their damage is more than skin-deep, however; many external parasites also carry serious, even deadly, systemic diseases.

Fleas

Fleas have long been the bane of dogs, but recent advances have finally put dog owners on the winning side in the fight against fleas. In any but the mildest of infestations, the new products available are well worth their initial higher purchase price. It's a lot cheaper to put an expensive product on your dog once every 3 months than to reapply a cheap one every day.

A red Smooth.

Always read the ingredients. You may think you're getting a deal with a less expensive product that is applied the same and boasts of the same results as one of the more expensive products, but you're not getting a deal if it doesn't contain the right ingredients. Some of the major ingredients in the newer products are
• *imidacloprid,* a liquid applied once a month on the animal's back. It gradually distributes itself over the entire skin surface and kills at least 98 percent of the fleas on the animal within 24 hours and will continue to kill fleas for a month. It can withstand water, but not repeated swimming or bathing.
• *fipronil,* which comes as either a spray that you must apply all over the dog's body or a self-distributing liquid applied only on the dog's back. Once applied, fipronil collects in the hair follicles and then wicks out over time. Thus, it is resistant to

being washed off and can kill fleas for up to 3 months on dogs. It is also effective on ticks for a shorter period.
• *lufenuron,* which is given as a pill once a month. Fleas that bite the dog and ingest the lufenuron in the dog's system are rendered sterile. All animals in the environment must be treated in order for the regime to be effective, however.

Traditional flea control products are either less effective or less safe than these newer products.

Ticks

Two newer products for tick control are amitraz collars (tick collars) and fipronil spray or liquid. Neither will keep ticks totally off your dog, but they may discourage them from staying or implanting. Even with these precautions, you should still use your hands to feel for ticks in your dogs whenever you are in a potentially tick-infested area.

Ticks can be found anywhere on the dog, but most often burrow around the ears, neck, and chest and between the toes. To remove a tick, use a tissue or tweezers, since some diseases can be transmitted to humans. Grasp the tick as close to the skin as possible, and pull slowly and steadily, trying not to leave the head in the dog. Don't squeeze the tick, as this can inject its contents into the dog. Clean the site with alcohol. Often a bump will remain after the tick is removed, even if you got the head. It will go away with time.

Ticks can transmit several serious diseases, especially ehrlichiosis, a potentially fatal disease that cripples the immune system. Symptoms may include lack of energy, dullness of coat, occasional vomiting, occasional loss of appetite, coughing, arthritis, muscle wasting, seizures, spontaneous bleeding, anemia, or a host of other nonspecific signs.

Mites

Mites are tiny organisms that are in the tick and spider family. Chemicals that are effective on fleas have no effect on mites. Of the many types of mites, only a few typically cause problems in dogs.

Sarcoptes mites cause sarcoptic mange, which causes intense itching, often characterized by scaling of the ear tips, and small bumps and crusts of other affected areas. Most of the lesions are found on the ear tips, abdomen, elbows, and hocks. Treatment requires repeated shampoos or dips of not only the affected dog, but other household pets that are in contact with the infected dog. It is highly contagious, even to humans, and spread by direct contact. Skin scrapings may reveal the responsible *Sarcoptes scabiei* mite. The presence of just one mite lends a definite diagnosis, but the absence of mites doesn't mean they aren't present.

Demodex mites cause demodectic mange. Unlike sarcoptic mange, it is not contagious and is not usually itchy. Most cases of demodectic mange appear in puppies, and most consist of only a few patches that

Spraying your dog with a flea and tick spray before venturing into woodland areas and tall grass and examining his coat afterward will greatly reduce your dog's chance of contracting external parasites.

often go away by themselves. This localized variety is not considered hereditary. In some cases it begins as a diffuse moth-eaten appearance, particularly around the lips and eyes, or on the front legs, or the dog has many localized spots. These cases tend to get worse until the dog has generalized demodectic mange. Demodectic mange affecting the feet is also common and can be extremely resistant to treatment.

Cheyletialla mites are contagious and cause mild itchiness. They look like small white specks in the dog's hair near the skin. Many flea insecticides also kill these mites, but they are better treated by using special shampoos or dips.

Ear Mites

Ear mites are primarily found in puppies or ill adults. An affected dog will scratch its ears, shake its head, and perhaps hold its head sideways. The ear mite's signature is a dark dry waxy buildup resembling coffee grounds in the ear canal, usually of both ears. Sometimes the tiny mites can be seen with a magnifying glass if the material is placed on a dark background.

Separate a dog with ear mites from other pets and wash your hands after handling its ears. Ideally, every pet in a household should be treated. Your veterinarian can provide the best medication. Because ear mites are also found in the dog's fur all over its body, you should also treat the dog's fur with a pyrethrin-based shampoo or spray.

Maintenance Care

Just as with people, grooming involves more than hair care.

Ear Care

The dog's ear canal is made up of an initial long vertical segment that then abruptly angles to run horizontally toward the skull. This configuration provides a moist environment in which various ear infections can flourish. Check your dog's ears regularly and don't allow moisture or debris to accumulate in them.

Ear problems can be difficult to cure once they have become established, so that early veterinary attention is crucial. Signs of ear problems include inflammation, discharge, debris, foul odor, pain, scratching, shaking, tilting of the head, or circling to one side. Bacterial and yeast infections, ear mites or ticks, foreign bodies, inhalant allergies, seborrhea, or hypothyroidism are possible underlying problems. Because the ear canal is lined with skin, any skin disorder that affects the dog elsewhere can also strike its ears. Grass awns are a common cause of ear problems in dogs that spend time outdoors. Keep the ear lubricated with mineral oil, and seek veterinary treatment as soon as possible.

If your dog has ear debris, but no signs of discomfort or itching, you can try cleaning the ear yourself, but be forewarned that overzealous cleaning can irritate the skin lining the ear canal. You can buy products to clean the ear or use a homemade mixture of one part alcohol to two parts white vinegar. Hold the ear near its base and quickly squeeze in the ear cleaner (the slower it drips, the more it will tickle). Gently massage the liquid downward and squish it all around. Then stand back and let your dog shake it all out (be sure you're outdoors). If the ear has so much debris that repeated rinses don't clean it right up, you have a problem that needs veterinary attention. If the ear is red, swollen, or painful, do not attempt to clean it yourself. Your dog may need to be sedated for cleaning, and may have a serious problem. Cleaning solutions will flush debris but will not kill mites or cure infections. Don't stick cotton swabs down in the ear canal, as they can irritate the skin and pack debris into the horizontal canal. Don't use powders in the ear, which can cake, or hydrogen peroxide, which can leave the ear moist.

Nail Care

Dachshund nails evolved to withstand strenuous running and digging. Unless your Dachshund is a marathon runner or digger, you'll need to trim his nails regularly. The most common problem associated with overly long nails happens when the nail becomes snagged on a tree root or even carpet loop, pulling the nail from its bed or dislocating the toe. In addition, overly long nails impact on the ground with every step,

causing discomfort and eventually splayed feet and lameness. If dew claws (the rudimentary "thumbs" on the wrists) are left untrimmed, they can get caught on things more easily and can be ripped out or actually loop around and grow into the dog's leg. You must prevent this by trimming your dog's nails every week or two.

It's easier to cut the nails by holding the foot backwards, much as a horse's hoof is held when being shod. This way your dog can't see what's going on, and you can see the bottom of the nail. You can also hold your dog in your lap on his back. Notice that the nail is thick near its base and suddenly tapers. Viewed from beneath, you will see a solid core culminating in a hollowed nail. Cut the tip up to the core or narrow area, but not beyond. On occasion you will slip up and cause the nail to bleed. Apply styptic powder to the nail to stop the bleeding. If this is

Snip off only the tip, avoiding the sensitive quick in the nail's core.

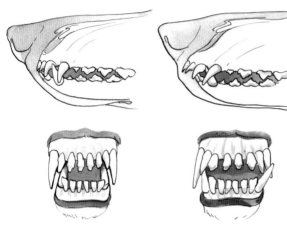

not available, dip the nail in flour or hold it to a wet tea bag. And be more careful next time!

Dental Care

Between 4 and 7 months of age, Dachshund puppies will shed their baby teeth and show off new permanent teeth. Often deciduous (baby) teeth, especially the canines (fangs), are not shed, so that the permanent tooth grows in beside the baby tooth. If this condition persists after the permanent teeth are fully in, consult your veterinarian. Retained baby teeth can cause misalignment of adult teeth. Correct occlusion is important for good dental health. In a correct Dachshund bite, the top incisors should fit snugly in front of the bottom incisors, with the top canines just behind the bottom canines. If the bottom canines are behind or opposed to the top canines, the bottom ones can be displaced inward and pierce the palate every time the mouth is closed.

Tooth plaque and tartar not only are unsightly but also contribute to bad breath and health problems. If not removed, plaque will attract bacteria and minerals, which will harden into tartar. Plaque can cause infections to form along the gum line, then spread rootward causing irreversible periodontal disease with tissue, bone, and tooth loss. The bacteria may also sometimes enter the bloodstream and cause infection in the kidneys and heart valves.

Dry food, and hard dog biscuits, carrots, rawhide, and dental chewies are only minimally helpful at removing plaque. Some prescription dog food contains ingredients that decrease tartar accumulation, but brushing your Dachshund's teeth with a dog toothpaste and brush is the best plaque remover. Most dogs are surprisingly cooperative. Your dog's teeth may have to be cleaned under anesthesia as often as once a year if you do not brush them.

A well-groomed Dachshund feels better, looks better, and has a head start on a long and healthy life. You wouldn't want any less for your Dachshund—even if he would rather be covered with dirt!

Chapter Seven
Dachshund Delinquents

When the world beckons with holes needing digging, clothes needing shredding, shoes needing chewing, cats needing chasing, trails needing following, what's a poor Dachshund to do? Even good Dachshunds, with good owners, do bad things.

Until recently even the best owners had little choice of where to turn for advice for dog behavior problems. Far too many Dachshunds have been relinquished because their owners never received adequate advice. Well-meaning but misguided training advice from friends, breeders, or even veterinarians or dog trainers without a scientific background in dog behavior too often only made things worse. Great strides have been made in recent years in canine behavioral therapy. Qualified behaviorists will consider both behavioral and medical therapies. As a first step in any serious behavior problem, a thorough veterinary exam should be performed.

Harsh or repeated punishment never helps teach your dog anything except to fear you. If punishment doesn't work the first time, why would it work the second, third, or fourth time?

House Soiling

If an adult soils inside, especially if she was formerly housetrained, a veterinary examination is warranted to consider the following possibilities:
• Older dogs may simply not have the bladder control that they had as youngsters; a doggy door is the best solution.
• Older spayed females may dribble urine, especially when sleeping; ask your veterinarian about drug therapies.
• Frequent urination of small amounts (especially if the urine is bloody or dark) may indicate an infection of the urinary tract. Such infections must be treated promptly.
• Increased urine production can be a sign of kidney disease or diabetes; your veterinarian can test for and treat these disorders. Never restrict water from these dogs; a doggy door is a better way to cope.
• Sometimes a housetrained dog will be forced to soil the house because

of a bout of diarrhea, and afterwards will continue to soil in the same area. If this happens restrict that area from the dog, deodorize the area with an enzymatic cleaner, and revert to basic housebreaking lessons.

• Male dogs may "lift their leg" inside of the house as a means of marking it as theirs. Castration will often solve this problem as long as it performed before the habit has become established; otherwise diligent deodorizing and the use of some dog-deterring odorants (available at pet stores) may help.

• Submissive dogs, especially young females, may urinate upon greeting you. Such "submissive urination" tends to be worse if you do anything to dominate or threaten the dog, so raising your voice or punishing or standing over the dog tends to bring on more urination. Try to greet such dogs calmly, kneeling down to their level. Submissive urination is usually outgrown as the dog gains more confidence.

If everything checks out normal, your best bet is to go back to the basics and begin housetraining as though she were a puppy (see page 34).

Some dogs defecate or urinate because of the stress of separation anxiety; you must treat the anxiety to cure the symptom. Dogs that mess their crate when left in it are usually suffering from separation anxiety or anxiety about being closed in a crate. Other tell-tale signs of anxiety-produced elimination are drooling, scratching, and escape-oriented behavior. You need to treat separation anxiety and start crate training over, placing the dog in it for a short period of time and working up gradually to longer times. Dogs that suffer from crate claustrophobia but not separation anxiety do better if left loose in a dog-proofed room or yard.

Home Destruction

One of the joys of dog ownership is that no matter what you've done, the one family member you can count on being overwhelmed with joy at your return home is your dog. The joyous reunion is greatly diminished, however, if you are overwhelmed by the sight of your vandalized home. The vandal is your loving Dachshund, telling you how much she loves you as only a Dachshund can do.

When a calm adult destroys your home, she is likely destroying out of anxiety, not spite. Being left alone is an extremely stressful situation for these highly social animals. They react by becoming agitated and trying to escape from confinement, digging and chewing around doors and windows, hyperventilating, salivating, and perhaps soiling the house. Punishing these dogs with separation anxiety is ineffective because it actually increases the anxiety level of the dog.

Keeping the dog crated may save your home, but it seldom deals with the problem. Some dogs urinate or defecate in their crates, rip up bedding, dig and bite at the cage door, bark, pant, shake, and drool.

Separation anxiety should be treated by leaving the dog alone for very short periods of time and gradually working to longer periods, taking care to never allow the dog to become anxious during any session. When you *must* leave your dog for long periods during the conditioning program, leave her in a different part of the house than the one in which the conditioning sessions take place. This way you won't undo all of your work if she becomes overstressed by your long absence.

When you return home, no matter how horrified or relieved you are at the condition of the house, greet your dog calmly. Then have her perform a simple trick or obedience exercise so that you have an excuse to praise her. In severe cases your veterinarian can prescribe antianxiety medications to help your pet deal with being left alone during the training process.

Some dogs destroy out of boredom. Puppies are natural demolition dogs, and they vandalize for the sheer ecstasy that only a search and destroy mission can provide. The best cure (besides old age) is supervision and prevention. Meanwhile, tiring them with both physical and mental exercise an hour or so before leaving can help. Puppies and many adults have a need to chew. Give them an assortment of chew toys to satisfy the urge. Several toys that can provide hours of entertainment are available; for example, some can be filled with peanut butter or treats in such a way that it takes the dog a

The patented Dachshund look of innocence.

very long time to extract the food from the toy.

Bad Manners

Is your Dachshund driving you crazy? Chances are, it's you who is driving her crazy by not giving her enough exercise. Make both of you happy and give her lots of mental and physical exercise. This means a good run, a fast paced game, or a challenging obedience lesson several times a day. A dog agility course is a great mind and body exerciser.

Jumping Up

Jumping up to greet you is a normal canine behavior, but it can be an

"Who me?"

irritating one. Teach your Dachshund to sit and stay so that you can kneel down to her level for greetings. When she does jump up, simply say *"No"* and step backward, so that her paws meet only air. Teaching your dog a special command that lets her know it's okay to jump up can actually help her discriminate the difference.

Don't just hustle her out of the room when guests come over, or she will only get more crazed to greet people and be more out of control when she finally gets the chance. The more people she gets a chance to greet politely, the less excited she'll be about meeting new people, and the less inclined to jump on them. This requires having friends that will work with you by kneeling and greeting your sitting Dachshund, and not allowing her to jump on them. Your Dachshund should learn that polite

dogs are greeted by guests, but impolite dogs are not. After greeting, have a special chew treat or toy for your dog to entertain herself with in the same room, so she learns to be part of the group without going crazy.

Barking

A Dachshund's bark is her best friend. She plays with it often. Don't begrudge your Dachshund's barking; it's part of her hunting heritage. That doesn't mean you should live with nonstop barking, however. Barking while hunting or playing, or at suspicious happenings around the home, are perfectly acceptable behaviors for most circumstances. Barking at falling leaves is not.

If your dog won't stop barking when you tell her to, distract her with a loud noise of your own. Begin to anticipate when your dog will start barking, distract her, and reward her for quiet behavior. You will actually create a better watchdog by discouraging your dog from barking at non-threatening objects and encouraging her to bark momentarily at suspicious people.

A dog stuck in a pen in the backyard will bark. What else is there to do? Isolated dogs will often bark through frustration or as a means of getting attention and alleviating loneliness. Even if the attention gained includes punishment, they continue to bark in order to obtain the temporary presence of the owner. The fault is not theirs; they should never have been banned to solitary confinement in the first place.

The simplest solution is to move the dog's quarters to a less isolated location. Let the dog in your house or fence in your entire yard. If barking occurs when you put your dog to bed, move her bed into your bedroom, or condition your dog by rewarding her for successively longer periods of quiet behavior. The distraction of a special chew toy, given only at bedtime, may help alleviate barking. Remember, a sleeping dog can't bark, so exercise can be a big help.

Digging

If you have visions of restoring your lawn to the lush green carpet you had before your Dachshund moved in—dream on. Dachshunds are natural-born diggers. The best you can do is to provide your Dachshund an acceptable place to dig and

Pica and Copraphagia

Dogs can eat a variety of strange things. Pica, the ingestion of nonfood items (such as wood, fabric, or soil) can be a problem is some dogs. Talk to your veterinarian about possible health problems that could contribute to these specific hungers and about possible problems that could result from eating these items. The most common and disturbing nonfood item eaten by dogs is feces. This habit, called coprophagia, has been blamed on boredom, stress, hunger, poor nutrition, and excessively rich nutrition, but none of these has proved a completely satisfactory explanation. Food additives that make the stool less savory are available, and you can also try adding hot pepper to the stool, but a determined dog will not be deterred. The best cure is immediate removal of all feces. Many puppies experiment with stool-eating but grow out of it.

Dachshunds dig—what did you expect?

One way to teach your Dachshund not to jump up on you when you don't want her to is to teach her to jump up on command.

to direct her to it whenever she begins digging in an off-limits area. Make her a sandbox and salt it with buried treasures to keep her digging attention confined.

Fearfulness

Even a brave Dachshund can develop illogical fears, or phobias. The most common are fears of strange people or dogs and fear of gunshots or thunder. The cardinal rule of working with a fearful dog is to never push it into situations that might overwhelm it. Some people erroneously think the best way to

deal with a scared dog is to inundate her with the very thing she's afraid of, until she gets used to it. This concept (called flooding) doesn't work because the dog is usually so terrified she never gets over her fear enough to realize the situation is safe.

Other owners try to reassure their dog by petting or holding her when scared. This only reinforces the behavior and often also convinces the dog that the owner is frightened as well. You want to maintain a jolly attitude and make your dog work for praise. The first step is to teach your dog a few simple commands; performing these exercises correctly gives you a reason to praise her and also increases her sense of security because she knows what's expected of her.

In some cases, the dog is petrified at even the lowest level of exposure to whatever she is scared of. You may have to use antianxiety drugs in conjunction with training to calm your dog enough to make progress.

Shyness

If a Dachshund is shy, don't let people push themselves on her. It frightens the dog, sometimes to the extent that the person could be bitten. Strangers should be asked to ignore shy dogs, even when approached by the dog. When the dog gets braver, have the stranger offer her a tidbit, at first while not even looking at the dog. It's not necessary for your dog to love strangers, but she should be comfortable enough with them so that she can be treated by a veterinarian, boarded, or caught if lost, without being emotionally traumatized.

Aggression

Many types of aggression can occur in dogs, and the treatment for them can be very different. Often new Dachshund owners have difficulty telling if their dog is actually behaving aggressively.

Is It Really Aggression?

Puppies and dogs play by growling and biting. Because many people have seen horror stories about aggressive dogs, they immediately label a puppy that growls and bites as a problem biter. You need to know the difference between true aggression and playful aggression. Look for these clues that tell you it's all in good fun:

• Wagging tail
• Down on elbows in front, with the rump in the air (the play-bow position)
• Barks intermingled with growls
• Lying down or rolling over
• Bounding leaps or running in circles
• Mouthing or chewing on you or other objects

On the other hand, look for these clues to know you better watch out:

• Low growl combined with a direct stare
• Tail held stiffly
• Sudden, unpredictable bites
• Growling or biting in defense of food, toys, or bed
• Growling or biting in response to punishment

Chances are your Dachshund is simply playing. Still, this doesn't mean you should let her use you as a chewstick. When your pup bites you simply say, *"Ouch! No!"* and remove your chomped body part from her mouth. Replace it with a toy. Hitting your dog is uncalled for—she was just trying to play. Hitting also is a form of aggression that could give your dog the idea that she had better bite harder next time because you're playing the game a lot rougher.

Aggressive behavior is usually not a sign of disease unless it is totally unprecedented. It can be a sign of pain, an endocrine problem, or a brain problem. Such dogs should be seen by a neurologist or a veterinarian specializing in behavior.

Aggression Toward Other Dogs

Life with more than one Dachshund is never dull. Problems between canine housemates are more likely to occur between dogs of the same sex and same age. Seniority counts for a lot in the dog world, and a young pup will usually grow up respecting his elders. Occasionally trouble will brew. While rough play and occasional flared tempers are natural, repeated disagreements that leave one dog screaming or bleeding, or in which the dogs cannot be readily separated, spell trouble. Neutering one or both males in a two-male dominance dispute can sometimes help, but neutering females seldom helps.

"Danger! Danger! Come and see!"

It's human nature to soothe the underdog and punish the bully, but you'd be doing the underdog no favor. If your dogs are fighting for dominance, they are doing so partly for your attention and favor. If you give it to the victim, the aggressor will only try harder to earn your attention by getting rid of the wrongful heir. Instead, treat the winning dog like a king and the losing dog like a prince. This means you always greet, pet, and feed the top dog first. That doesn't mean you reward either for fighting; if a fight breaks out, separate them as quickly as possible either by pulling them apart or by throwing some water on them. Express your displeasure and separate them for a short time. Reintroduce them soon after, and make sure they are both distracted with a treat or a chance to go on a walk.

Going for a long walk together in neutral territory, with each dog leashed, is an ideal way for dogs to get used to one another and associate the other with a pleasurable event. Prevent an aggressive dog from marking with urine during the walk. Dogs mark their territory by urinating on various posts; the more you allow a dog to mark, the more likely that dog will behave aggressively toward other dogs in that area.

Dachshunds think nothing of approaching and even challenging strange dogs with all the cockiness of a street fighter. This tough facade is often enough to scare away a big dog, but sometimes the other dog meets the challenge—not good news for most Dachshunds.

Aggression Toward Humans

Some Dachshunds have given the breed the reputation of being snappy with strangers. Most of them are just overexuberant watchdogs, but your guests will not be amused. Teach the dog some simple obedience exercises, including Sit and Stay. Reward her for sitting and staying around strangers, and have the strangers also reward her. Sometimes practicing in a neutral location will help. You may need to have her wear a muzzle if she might bite.

Dominance aggression is not common but can occur when your Dachshund considers herself your boss. She may growl or bite if you try to remove food or a toy, encroach on her sleeping quarters, or step past her in a narrow hall or during a perceived display of dominance by you (such as petting, grooming, scolding, or leading). Punishment usually only elicits further aggression. Dominance aggression is more common in males than females, and occasionally (but not always) castration can help.

Owners of such dogs inevitably feel guilty, and wonder "Where did I go wrong?" The fault is not entirely theirs. Although some actions of the owner may have helped create the problem, these same actions would not have produced dominance aggression in dogs that were not already predisposed to the problem. In predisposed dogs, owners who act in ways to foster the dog's opinion of herself as queen can lead to problems. What would convince a dog that she ranked over a person? Actions such as:

• Petting the dog on demand

• Feeding the dog before eating your own meal
• Allowing the dog to go first through doorways
• Allowing the dog to win at games
• Allowing the dog to have her way when she acts aggressively
• Fearing the dog
• Not correcting the dog for initial instances of aggression

Treatment consists of no longer doing these behaviors. Your dominant aggressive dog must earn her treats and pets by doing simple obedience exercises. You call the shots, not your Dachshund. It's best to avoid situations that might lead to a showdown. If, however, your dog only growls, and *never* bites, you may be able to nip the behavior in the bud before you get nipped yourself by scolding or banning the dog from the room. If your dog is likely to bite, but you still want to try, talk to your veterinarian about temporary drug therapy to calm it sufficiently during initial training, and consider having your dog wear a muzzle.

As with people, dogs can develop an astounding array of behavioral problems. No dog, and no owner, is perfect. Our dogs seldom act and do exactly as we would wish them to; we probably let them down even more. We try to change what we can, gripe about the rest, and love them regardless because the good more than makes up for the bad.

Chapter Eight
The Educated Dachshund

Dachshunds have a good mind to do something. The problem is, they're not always that particular about whether you consider that something good or bad. Their inquisitive psyches seek out challenges and entertainment, and unless you give them something constructive to do, they can just as likely turn their talents to destructive demonstrations. The choice is yours.

With some direction in the form of training, you can direct your Dachshund's brain power toward good rather than evil. You can train your Dachshund as much or as little as you want. Every dog should know how to come when called, stay when told, and walk nicely at your side. You can be satisfied with this or ask for more and more. You can even demonstrate your Dachshund's genius at several types of trials. The main objective is to interact with your dog in a positive and stimulating way every day. Not only will he have better manners because of what you teach him, but he will also have better

"Next time she tells you to sit, here's what you do . . ."

manners because he has learned to learn, and because you have shown him the way toward better teamwork.

Training won't dampen your Dachshund's spirit, as long as you train the right way. Training the right way means nurturing the bond between you and your dog by helping him understand what you are trying to tell him. It means making learning exciting and rewarding by incorporating play and using lots of toys and treats for rewards. Forget the old-fashioned push, pull, choke, and dominate school of dog training. Dachshunds can always win in a battle of the wills. He may go through the motions, but you will not have achieved the goal of improving your relationship. To get a thinking dog to do what you want, and to do it consistently, it has to be what he wants. What does a Dachshund want? Fun. Your Dachshund will learn best when his tail is working as fast as his mind. That doesn't mean he never gets corrected—just that corrections should be fair, mild, and informative.

Fun means more than just games, although Dachshunds love to play.

"Please have mercy…"

Fun for Dachshunds includes chomping down some good treats. Treats can be used both to guide and reward when training. Just because you train with treats doesn't mean you are sentenced to carrying a pocket full of liver for the rest of your life. Once your Dachshund learns how to do something, you gradually wean him from getting a reward each time, instead rewarding only at random for correct responses. This random payoff keeps him thinking that next time just might be payoff time—the same psychology used to induce people to put money into slot machines over and over without constant reward.

Food isn't the only reward for your Dachshund. He's not a machine, but a dog that revels in the loving touch and appreciative voice of his special person. Heaping on praise, giving a hearty neck scratch, throwing a toy, or going for a romp are just as powerful incentives for many Dachshunds.

Whatever makes your Dachshund happiest is the best reward for him.

Tools of the Trade

The secret of training is not in the tools; it's in the trainer. Still, having the right tools can make things easier. Basic training equipment usually includes both short (6 foot) and long (about 20 foot) lightweight leads and a collar. Traditionally a slip (choke) collar has been used, but you can also use a buckle collar. If you use a slip collar, be sure to put it on correctly, with the "live" ring (the one your leash is attached to that slips through the other, "dead," ring) coming from your dog's left side over his neck to you on his right. That way it will tighten and loosen correctly. It's not for choking your dog, or for hurting your dog at all, which is why many trainers feel better using a buckle collar. Never leave a choke collar on your dog when he's unattended; it could get caught on something and really choke him.

Short dogs can be tiring to train. You can avoid some of the bending by teaching your dog stationary exercises on a raised surface. Some people use a grooming table, others use a chair or bed. Professional dog trainers tend to use a slightly elevated stand the dog comes to associate with training.

Another problem with short dogs is that no matter how you try to guide them with the leash the leash mostly just pulls upward. By stringing your leash through a section of narrow PVC pipe you can move the pipe and so guide your dog left or right, forward and backward.

Another small dog tool is a lightweight stick that you can use to point to where you want your Doxie to face. You can use a long spoon with peanut butter or squeeze cheese plastered on the end of it. Your dog will learn that when he follows the spoon he gets a reward. Other trainers prefer to use a lightweight stick as an extension for their own hands, so they can gently tap (not hit!) or guide the dog into position without bending over every time. Of course, you

can ignore these aids and look upon training time as a free calisthenics class.

Clicks for Tricks

Clicker training is an effective training technique that's been used for decades to train performance animals, especially dolphins. It works just as well for dogs. In clicker training you teach the dog that the sound of a clicker (a device available from most pet stores and catalogs) signals a reward is coming. A clicker signal is used because it is fast, noticeable, and something the dog otherwise does not encounter in everyday life. You can substitute another novel sound. The first step is to just click and reward your dog with tiny tidbits, several zillion times, for no reason except that the dog eventually looks at you. Since Dachshunds are pretty clever when it comes to predicting food, they may take only a few repetitions to learn the association.

Once the dog associates the click with

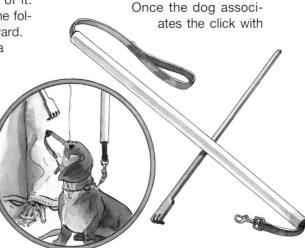

A long stick or backscratcher can help you reach your dog without bending over so far, and a solid leash (a piece of PVC with a leash through it) can help you guide your dog in directions other than up.

The Rules

- *Guide, don't force.* Forcing Dachshunds can cause them to resist, actually slowing down learning. It's also not healthy for dogs with back or joint problems.
- *Smart dogs are thinking dogs.* Give your dog a chance to work problems out rather than rushing him to make a response. He will be able to cope with new situations better if he hasn't learned by rote.
- *Give your dog a hunger for learning.* Your Dachshund will work better if his stomach is not full, and will be more responsive to food rewards. Never try to train a sleepy, tired, sick, or hot dog.
- *Be a quitter.* You and your dog have good days and bad days. On bad days, quit. Never train your dog when you are irritable or impatient. Even on good days, don't push it. After about 15 minutes your dog's performance will begin to suffer unless a lot of play is involved. Keep your Dachshund wanting more.

- *Have a dog's eye view.* If your Dachshund just doesn't seem to "get it" or seems stubborn, stop. Chances are if what you're doing hasn't worked so far, repeating it over and over won't work either. Think about what his perception of the situation is. You may need to back up and give him simpler steps, or make sure he's having fun, or let him have a chance to make his own decisions.
- *Play tricks!* Sit, Down, Stay, and Heel can be pretty boring after a while. Add a few fun tricks, and your Dachshund will be more likely to think all training is fun.
- *Your Dachshund didn't read the book.* Nothing ever goes as perfectly as it does in training instructions. Although there may be setbacks, you can train your dog, as long as you remember to be consistent, gentle, realistic, and patient—and have a good sense of humor!

an upcoming reward, you wait for or induce the dog to do the behavior you want. The instant he does so, you click to tell him his behavior is going to pay off. If he makes a mistake, nothing happens. You just wait for him to do it right, giving him guidance when possible. In essence, the dog thinks he's training you because he realizes whenever he does a certain behavior he makes you click and then reward him.

Timing

Timing is important in any training, but especially clicker training. The crux of training is anticipation: the dog comes to anticipate that after hearing a command, he will be rewarded if he performs some action, and he will eventually perform this action without further assistance from you. Correct timing goes like this:

1. *Name.* Alert your dog that your next words are directed toward him by preceding commands with his name.

2. *Command.* Always use the same word in the same tone.

3. *Action.* Don't simultaneously place the dog into position as you say the command, which negates the predictive value of the command. Instead, give the dog time to assimilate your command and then help him to perform the desired action.

4. *Reward.* As soon as possible after the dog has performed correctly should come a signal *("Good!")* followed by a reward.

The sooner a reward follows an action, the better the association. It's sometimes difficult to reward a dog instantly, though, and that's where clicker training comes in.

Here's how to use a clicker to train your Doxie, named Moxie, to sit. First click and then reward Moxie many times so he realizes a click means a treat is coming his way. Once he's looking to you expectantly at the sound of the click you can start real training. Lure his front up by holding a treat above and behind his muzzle. If he jumps up for it, take it away. Only when he bends his rear legs do you click, and reward. Do it again, clicking and rewarding for successively closer approximations to the sit position. When he gets the idea, add the command "sit" before luring him into position. Then gradually fade out the lure. You can use the same concept to teach Moxie to lie down, come, heel, bark, crawl on his belly, roll over, or do anything he naturally does on his own. And he

still will think he's training you—and what Dachshund wouldn't like that idea!

New Dogs, Old Tricks

You can teach an old dog new tricks, but it's better to teach a young dog old tricks. Those old tricks are Sit, Come, Stay, Down, and Heel.

Come

The most important command your Dachshund can learn is to come when called. It's also sometimes the hardest. With so many enticing scents and sights, how do you make your Dachshund leave what he's

Dachshunds can be good!

Small dogs can present training challenges.

doing to see what you want? You make sure he knows that coming to you is always more rewarding than whatever he could possibly find elsewhere. And you make sure he never is scolded—no matter how much you feel like chastising him for whatever mischief he's just caused—when he comes. Smart Dachshunds learn that when they're bad, they can come running up to you when called and get total forgiveness and a delicious treat. Smart Dachshund trainers let them get away with that ruse. At least they're coming.

To train your Dachshund to come enthusiastically, have a helper gently restrain him while you back away, enticing him with treats or baby talk until he is struggling to get to you. Then excitedly call *"Moxie, come!"* and turn and run away. Your helper

should immediately release him. If you are clicker training, you can click while he's still on his way to you. When he catches you, give him a special reward and make him feel like the smartest dog on the planet. Keep up a jolly attitude and make him feel lucky to be part of such a wonderful game.

Next let Moxie meander around, and in the midst of his investigations, call, run backwards, and reward him when he runs to you. Again, you can click just as soon as he heads toward you. If he ignores you, attach a light line and give him a very gentle tug to guide him to you immediately after you call. After a few repetitions, drop the long line, let him mosey around a bit, and then call. If he begins to come, run away and let him chase you as part of the game. If he doesn't come, pick up the line

A properly trained Dachshund will enjoy his lessons.

and give a tug, then run away as usual. As your dog becomes more reliable, you should begin to practice (still on the long line) in the presence of distractions. Hold onto his leash just in case the distractions prove too enticing.

Some dogs develop a habit of dancing around just out of your reach, considering your futile grabs to be another part of this wonderful game. You can prevent this by requiring Moxie to allow you to hold him by the collar before you click or reward him. Eventually you may add sitting in front of you as part of the game. In an obedience trial, a dog must sit in front of you within touching distance in order to pass the recall exercise; points are deducted for not sitting directly in front of you. In real life, however, you just want him to come!

Stay

Bolting through an open door is a potentially deadly habit. Teach your dog to sit and stay until given the release signal before exiting the car or house.

Have your dog sit, then say *"Stay"* in a soothing voice (you can omit the dog's name here, because many dogs jump up in anticipation when they hear their name—the opposite of what you want them to do!). If he tries to get up or lie down, gently but instantly place him back into position. Work up to a few seconds, give a click, then reward. Then give him a release word *("Okay!")* so he knows he can get up. After he masters sitting still for a few seconds, have him stay and then step out (starting with your right foot) and turn to stand directly in front of him. Step out with your right foot because when training for heeling, you will step off on your left foot—the foot nearest your dog—so he can use that as a heeling cue. Have him stay for a few seconds, and then step back beside him, click, and reward. You may have faster results if you train him on an elevated surface that dissuades him from following you, but don't place him where he could leap down and injure himself if he decides to take off.

It's tempting to stare into your dog's eyes as if hypnotizing him to stay, but staring is perceived by dogs as a threat, intimidating them so they come to you in appeasement. Work up to longer times, but don't ask a young puppy to stay longer than 30 seconds. The object is not to push your dog to the limit, but to let him succeed. Finally, practice with the dog on lead by the front door or in the car. Don't tease him; reward him with a walk or a car ride!

Down

It may be only a few inches difference between sitting and lying down, but those few inches can be tough ones if you try to force them. Having a dog that will lie down when asked to makes it easier to take the dog visiting or to ask the dog to stay in one place. It's also handy for grooming or examining your dog.

Begin with Moxie sitting. Move a treat below his nose toward the ground. If he reaches down to get it, click, then give it to him. Repeat, requiring him to reach farther down (without lifting his rear from the ground) until he must lower his elbows to the ground. Don't try to cram his down position, which can scare a submissive dog and cause a dominant dog to resist. Once he has the idea, add the signal "Moxie, down" before luring him.

Heel

Walking on a leash should always be a good experience. If he's just starting leash training, attach a lightweight leash and simply follow him around at first. Occasionally show him some food and encourage him to walk toward it. Then have him walk next to you for a few steps as he goes for the food. You can also click and praise as he walks with you.

Many Dachshunds suddenly turn into canine anchors when first put on leash. Some are used to being carried, but most just don't like the idea of being restrained. Resist the urge to drag him! Change directions and give him a goal. If he wants to go home, carry him to the end of the driveway and let him lead you home. If he wants food, walk to the kitchen on lead and give him a treat. If he wants adventure, walk around the block or to the park. Along the way play human snack machine and dole out the treats for walking where you want to go.

Dachshunds are great at tripping you, so once your dog is walking on lead, you should teach him to walk in a Heel position. Even if you have no intention of teaching a perfect competition "Heel," he should know how to walk politely at your side. Have him

A well-trained Dachshund will stay just about anywhere when asked.

sit in Heel position; that is, on your left side with his neck parallel with your leg. If you line up your feet and your dog's front feet, that's close enough. Step off with your left foot. During your first few practice sessions keep him on a short lead, holding him in Heel position, and giving him a click of approval—and, of course, praise and treats. As he gets the idea, you can let out more lead, clicking and praising and rewarding when he is in Heel position. The outdated method of letting a dog lunge to the end of the lead and then snapping him back is unfair to any dog if you haven't first shown him what you expect, and it is dangerous for a Dachshund. Think like a dog: Wouldn't you rather learn something if somebody showed you what was expected first rather than learn something by being punished for something you were never shown?

Keep up a brisk pace so he doesn't have time to sniff and sightsee. Add some about-faces, right and left turns, and changes in speed. You can teach him to sit every time you stop. Your dog doesn't always have to heel when on lead, but be sure to give the *"Okay"* command before allowing him to sniff, forge, and meander.

Higher Education

Your well-behaved Dachshund can Sit, Down, Stay, Come, and Heel. Although useful, these exercises aren't exactly mentally stimulating, and he's likely to get bored with them. He may relish the chance to do more active exercises than those involved in basic obedience. You can spice up training by adding some more challenging exercises right from the start.

Obedience training, like other activities, can bring you and your dog even closer together.

Several advanced exercises require high and broad jumping. High jumping with a Dachshund means 8 inches, but you can practice with lower jumps. Other advanced exercises require retrieving special obedience dumbbells and gloves, and the sooner you get these items, the more likely your Dachshund will enjoy carrying them. The most advanced exercises involve hand signals and scent discrimination. Again, there is no reason to postpone introducing these concepts to your dog. Teach hand signals just as you would voice signals; if your dog already knows voice signals, add hand signals by immediately preceding your standard voice command with a signal.

For scent discrimination, train your dog to sniff out hidden objects with your scent on them. Throw a scented object in the midst of several unscented objects that are tied down (you can have a friend tie them down or tie them yourself while wearing gloves to diminish your scent on them). Your dog will learn that only the article with your fresh scent can be picked up.

Class Acts

Good obedience classes are great aids for training your dog to behave properly at home, in public, and in competition. To find a good class, get referrals from other Dachshund trainers and sit in on the class. If the class uses outdated yank and jerk methods, look elsewhere. Your friend's well-being is worth too much.

If you plan on going on to compete in obedience, a class is a necessity. Obedience trials are held amidst great distractions. It would be nearly impossible for your dog to pass without having some experience working around other dogs. Obedience classes are filled with people who share many of your same interests. If you take the plunge into competition, class is a place to celebrate wins and laugh about failures.

Sometimes your Dachshund will be the star pupil. Sometimes he will be the class clown. Each dog progresses at his own pace; every dog will improve, and many dogs will profit from repeating the same class after using the first time through as a warm-up.

Obedience classes train you to train your dog. Don't let your dog down. Remember, there's no such thing as an untrainable dog, only untrained dogs—and whose fault is that?

Dachshund Good Citizens

Your Dachshund comes when you call—eventually. He stays when told to—sort of. He heels—or at least doesn't trip you. Okay, so he may not be a drill team icon, but he's the kind of dog that's a pleasure to take out in public, the kind of dog that gives dogs a good name. He's a canine good citizen, and AKC offers a certificate to prove it. All he has to do is

• Accept a friendly stranger without acting shy or resentful, or breaking position to approach.

• Sit politely for petting by a stranger without acting shy or resentful.

• Allow examination of his ears, feet, and coat, along with gentle brushing, by a stranger without acting shy or resentful. He should be clean, groomed, and in reasonably proper weight.

• Walk politely on a loose leash, turning and stopping with you. He need not be perfectly aligned with you, but he shouldn't pull you along.

• Walk on a leash through a group of at least three other people without jumping on them, pulling, or acting overly exuberant, shy, or resentful.

• Sit and lie down on command (you can gently guide him into position) and then stay as you walk 20 feet away and back.

• Stay and then come to you when called from 10 feet away.

• Behave politely to another dog and handler team, showing only causal interest in them.

• React calmly to distractions such as a dropped chair or passing jogger without panicking, barking, or acting aggressively.

• Remain calmly when held by a stranger while you're out of sight for 3 minutes.

• Refrain from eliminating, growling, snapping, biting, or attempting to attack a person or dog while being evaluated.

Bring his buckle or slip collar, brush or comb, leash, and proof of rabies vaccination. All the tests are done on lead; a long line is provided for the Stay and Recall exercises. If your dog passes, he will receive a Canine Good Citizen certificate from the AKC.

Obedience Trials

You may not think of your Dachshund as being particularly obedient, but compared to most other hounds, he's a prodigy. Dachshunds earn more obedience titles than any other dogs in the AKC Hound group. True,

Well-trained Dachshunds can accompany you to many places and make a good impression of the breed.

part of this is because they are a popular breed, but part of it is because, given the right motivation, Dachshunds can do just about anything. Their quick reactions, alert demeanor, and aptitude for learning make them dazzling, if sometimes comical, obedience competitors. But don't expect mindless subservience; the independent Dachshund's idea of obedience is a team effort, not a master–slave relationship. Obedience should be fun. You won't pass every trial, so enjoy the times your dog does something imaginative enough to fail. Those are the stories you'll tell your friends and remember in the years to come.

You can tell your friends all you want how smart your Dachshund is, but if you really want to prove it, you can enter obedience trials and earn

titles attesting to his brilliance. His ability to perform a set group of exercises will be evaluated against a perfect performance, but he need not be perfect to pass. The beginning exercises include heeling, standing, and staying while being touched by the judge; coming when called; and staying while sitting and then lying down. This may not sound so hard, but in the midst of sights, sounds, and smells of a dog show, it's easy for an inquisitive Dachshund to get distracted.

The AKC offers successively more challenging levels of competition. To earn each title a dog must qualify at three trials. Each qualifying score requires passing every exercise and earning a total score of at least 170 points out of a possible 200 points. The classes and titles are

• *Novice* classes lead to the Companion Dog (CD) title. Exercises are heeling on-lead and off-lead (sitting automatically each time you stop, making right, left, and about turns, and changing to a faster and slower pace), heeling on-lead in a figure eight around two people, standing still off-lead 6 feet away from you and allowing a judge to touch him, coming to you when called from 20 feet away, and staying in a sitting position for 1 minute and a Down position for 3 minutes with a group of other dogs while you are 20 feet away.

• *Open* classes lead to the Companion Dog Excellent (CDX) title. The dog must heel off-lead (including a figure eight), come when called but drop to a Down position when told to do so, retrieve a thrown dumbbell both over a flat surface and over a high jump, jump over a broad jump, and stay in a sitting position for 3 minutes and a Down position for 5 minutes with a group of dogs while you are out of sight.

• *Utility* leads to the Utility Dog (UD) title. To earn a UD, a dog must Heel, Stay, Sit, Down, and Come in response to hand signals; retrieve both a leather and a metal article scented by the handler from among four other unscented articles; retrieve a glove designated by the handler from among three gloves in different locations; stop and stand while heeling and allow the judge to examine him with the handler standing 10 feet away, trot away from the handler for about 40 feet until told to stop and then turn and sit and then jump over one of two jumps designated by the handler.

• The Utility Dog Excellent (UDX) is awarded to dogs that earn ten legs in both Open and Utility classes at the same trials after earning the UD.

• The Obedience Trial Champion (OTCH) is awarded to dogs with UD titles that earn such high scores in Open or Utility classes that they defeat a large number of dogs.

A *Pre-Novice* class leading to the Pre-Novice (PN) title may soon be offered as well. In PN, all exercises are done on lead. Exercises are heeling in a giant figure eight pattern, sitting while the judge touches him, coming when called, and staying for 1 minute in a Sit position and 1 minute in a Down position with the handler 6 feet away. This class is judged on a pass/fail basis. This title is still in the planning stage as of publication.

The United Kennel Club (UKC) also offers obedience awards. Its requirements are similar to AKC obedience titles. The UKC awards the U-CD, U-CDX, U-UD, and U-OCH.

Dachshunds are smart, but they have their own set of hardships. Tall or wet grass can make some outdoor trials difficult for miniature Dachshunds. That Dachshund nose is never far away from the ground and all its enticing scents. Precision heeling by your side is difficult for tiny dogs. Unlike large dogs that can take their position cues from your torso, miniature Dachshunds must either heel while looking at you instead of where they are stepping or

Dachshunds of Distinction

• The first Dachshund OTCH was also the first hound OTCH: OTCH Mayrhofen Olympischer Star L, TD. "Gretl" won Top Dog at the prestigious Obedience World Series in 1978.

• American and Canadian Ch. and OTCH Ch. Himark Vanquish UDT was the first Dachshund to be both a conformation and obedience champion. The UDT indicates he was also a Tracking Dog.

• Can. OTCH, U-UD Ginger Snap Cookie Pindor, UDX, CG was the first UDX Dachshund. A mini-Smooth rescue, she had initially enrolled in obedience classes because her owners couldn't housetrain her!

• In terms of longevity, it would be hard to best Can. OTCH Owl Farms Sly Star ML, Am. UDX, CG, GER BH. "Minnie" earned her UD title at 2 years of age and was still competing at the age of 12. Along the way she was the top obedience Dachshund in the country.

• DC Owl Farms I Wanna be a Star ML, CDX, JE was ranked the #1 hound in obedience in 2001.

entertainment. Besides, there's not much difference between a Sit/Stay and Down/Stay when you're a Dachshund! Smaller Dachshunds are at a disadvantage compared to larger ones, because the distances and minimal jump heights (8 inches) are the same. But since when did a Dachshund let size stand in its way?

Rally!

Rally is a less regimented style of obedience in which you and your dog follow a course along which various signs tell you what to do next. The directions include things such as "sit," "take a step to the side," "spiral," and "jump." Three levels are offered: novice, advanced, and excellent. You can praise and talk to your dog throughout. The dog's willingness and enjoyment is more important in scoring than is precision. That part's not hard—rally obedience is fun!

Mind Games

Dachshunds like obedience, but they love other competitions that challenge both their minds and bodies.

Agility

Where else can a Dachshund run through tunnels, scurry across bridges, weave between poles, and, soar (sort of) over jumps—and not get in trouble for it?

Agility competition combines obedience, athleticism, and, most of all, excitement as dogs tackle an obstacle course in a race against time. The

try to cue from your moving lower legs. To look up at your face, it's more comfortable for them to be out from your side. A judge looming over a small dog for the stand for exam can be intimidating. Dachshunds find the Stay exercises boring and may decide to leave in search of better

Classes help your Dachshund learn how to behave around other dogs.

AKC, North American Agility Dog Council (NADAC), United States Dog Agility Association (USDAA) and United Kennel Club sponsor agility trials and award titles. Classes are divided by height, with Dachshunds in AKC competitions competing in the 8-inch jump height class for dogs 10 inches and under at the withers.

Your job is to guide your Dachshund from obstacle to obstacle, while he's off leash, without touching him or the obstacles or using any food or devices. The obstacles include an A-frame made of two long wide boards with their peak about 5 feet high; a dog walk made of a long narrow board suspended about 4 feet high; a seesaw; an open tunnel made of a long, wide, curving tube; a closed tunnel made of a lightweight fabric chute; and weave poles, as well as a number of jumps: single, double, and triple bar jumps, solid jump, broad jump, tire jump, and window jump. A pause table is also included, on which the dog must sit still for 5 seconds. The obstacles are arranged in different configurations from trial to trial. Dogs lose points for refusing an obstacle, knocking down a jump, missing a contact zone, taking obstacles out of sequence, or exceeding the allotted time limit. To get a qualifying score, a dog must earn 85 out of a possible 100 points with no nonqualifying deductions.

These mind games sound like fun!

Agility is a demanding sport, and your Dachshund should be in proper weight and good health before attempting it. High jumping and vigorous weaving can impose stresses on immature bones, so these should be left until adulthood; it can also stress arthritic dogs and especially those predisposed to intervertebral disk disease.

Dachshunds of Distinction
Two Dachshunds have earned the MACH title: Ginger (MACH Jackie Brink V Dorndorf CDX TD), followed by Bart (MACH Bartholomew Ray TD NAC NGC V-OJC FD).

Agility with a small dog presents special challenges. The more strides a dog takes between obstacles, the more chances he has to get distracted or turn elsewhere. Handlers must keep up a lively pace but remain close enough to stay in the dog's field of view—not always an easy compromise to make! The tunnels might seem easy, but they have ridges that can trip a tiny dog. Obstacles such as weave poles make little sense to small dogs because there's so much space between them the dog loses contact with them when weaving.

AKC Classes. AKC agility is divided into the standard agility classes that include all the obstacles, and the faster-paced Jumpers With Weaves (JWW) classes that emphasize jumping and speed. Titles for the standard agility classes are NA for Novice, OA for Open, AX for Excellent, and MX for Master. JWW titles are the same with a "J" added to the end (NAJ, OAJ, AXJ, and MXJ). The Master Agility Champion (MACH) title is the ultimate designation of superior performance, and is obtained by winning 750 championship points and 20 double qualifying scores from the Excellent Standard and Jumpers With Weaves classes.

Flyball
Dachshunds aren't the typical flyball breed, but since when were Dachshunds typical at anything? If your dog likes to run, jump, and, especially, catch tennis balls, this may be his event. Flyball is a relay

AKC Agility Classes

• The *Novice* class uses 13 to 15 obstacles, including the A-frame, pause table, dog walk, open tunnel, seesaw, closed tunnel, broad jump, panel jump, bar jump, double bar jump, tire jump, and weave poles, plus some additional bar jumps and tunnels.

• The *Open* class uses 16 to 18 obstacles, including the 12 mandatory obstacles from the Novice class and the triple bar jump.

• The *Excellent* class uses 18 to 20 obstacles, including all the Open class obstacles plus additional jumps or tunnels, all in a more complex layout than the lower classes.

For Jumpers With Weaves classes:
• The *Novice JWW* class uses 13 to 15 obstacles, including one double bar jump, one series of six weave poles, and an assortment of tunnels and bar jumps.

• The *Open JWW* class uses 16 to 18 obstacles, including one double bar jump, one triple bar jump or broad jump, one series of 6 to 12 weave poles, and an assortment of tunnels and bar jumps.

• The *Excellent JWW* class uses 18 to 20 obstacles, one double bar jump, one triple bar jump, one series of 9 to 12 weave poles, and an assortment of tunnels and bar jumps.

race in which two teams of four dogs each go head to head down a course of four low hurdles toward a box. The box shoots out a tennis ball when the dog triggers its spring-loaded platform. The dog catches the ball and heads back to the starting line so his teammate can start. The hurdle height is set at 4 inches below the shoulder height of the shortest dog on the team (down to 8-inch hurdles). Teams like having a small dog so they can have low hurdles, although Dachshunds are pushing this! Since this is a team sport, dogs earn points toward titles based on their team's times. Teammates accumulate points toward the Flyball Dog (FD), then the Flyball Dog Excellent (FDX), then Flyball Dog Champion (FDCH), Flyball Master (FM), and a couple more that no Dachshund has achieved—yet. But a caveat: some dogs can get injuries from twisting while catching, and Dachshunds can get knocked over by large dogs that run off course.

Dances with Dachshunds

How about a Fido do-si-do? Dancing with your dog, also called musical freestyle, allows you to choreograph dance steps in which your dog heels on either side, winds between your legs as you walk, twirls, bows, and performs any other moves the two of you create, all in step to music. And you get to lead!

Several organizations sponsor doggy dancing, or canine musical

Agility requires lots of jumping!

freestyle, competitions. Some competitions emphasize heelwork to music, more like cheek-to-cheek ballroom dancing. Others encourage more intricate and dazzling steps, often at a distance from one another, more like modern dance. Several Dachshunds have proved that dancers with two left feet can excel!

Off to the Races

Many Dachshunds will give chase to small objects dragged along the ground, and, in what once seemed like some good-hearted fun, they were encouraged to chase such objects in races against one another as entertainment at Greyhound tracks. The problem is that Dachshunds aren't built to be race dogs, and encouraging the activity with dogs that may not be physically up for it is not promoting good Dachshund health. Just as bad, some people began breeding Dachshunds for the ability to win at these events, producing very un-Dachshund-like Dachshunds. The Dachshund Club of America has issued an official statement against racing Dachshunds at promotional events.

Tricks

Dachshunds enjoy learning tricks, sometimes the sillier the better. And let's face it: your friends would rather see some dazzling Dachshund demonstration than they would your dog performing a (yawn) Down/Stay. The best tricks are the ones unique to your dog. If your dog has an endearing behavior, make up a cute command and slip it in when he looks like he's going to be doing his trick, and give him a good reward when he does it. You can teach him to bring you your slippers, take a bow, ring a bell to go out, or some of the more common dog tricks. Use the same concepts you used to teach other exercises. If it's a complicated trick, teach the last part of the trick first and work backward toward the beginning.

• Teach Roll Over by starting with your dog on her back. Say *"Roll over"* and let him go, luring him to an upright position with a treat. Be consistent in having him roll in one direction. Once he's doing that, start with him not quite on his back, but lying a bit on the side opposite of the side he needs to roll toward. Lure him over and reward him. Continue until he is starting in an upright position.

• Teach Catch by tossing a tidbit or soft toy in an arc toward your dog's nose. Snatch it off the ground before he can reach it. Eventually he'll real-

ize that to beat you to the bounty he'll have to catch it in mid-air!

• Teach Shake Hands to your sitting dog by saying *"Shake"* and holding a treat in your closed hand in front of him. Some dogs will pick up a foot to paw at your hand, but for most you have to nudge one leg, or lure his head far to one side so he has to lift the leg up on the opposite side. As soon as the paw leaves the ground, click and reward! Then require him to lift it higher and longer.

• Teach Speak by saying *"Speak"* when it appears your Doxie is about to bark. Then click and reward. Don't reward barking unless you've first said *"Speak"* or you could create a barking monster!

Whether you teach your dog tricks, obedience, agility, or dancing, teach him something. A Dachshund mind is a terrible thing to waste.

Chapter Nine

Dachshunds Down and Dirty

Sniffing, barking, and leading the way through the wilds—your Dachshund makes every walk around the block an imaginary hunt. Some Dachshunds get a chance to go further afield, using their acute scenting ability to track, their good sense to stay on the right trail, their melodious bays to keep you in touch, and their unflinching courage to face whatever's at the end of the trail—or deep within the earth.

Tracking

True to her hound heritage, your Dachshund has an acute sense of smell that enables her to follow a scent trail, find lost objects, and even sniff out contraband. Her natural inclination is to use her nose when she feels like it, usually to root out moles, pilfer your picnic basket, or check which neighborhood dogs have used the same route lately.

All she needs is some direction, and she will gladly use her nose to follow a human scent trail. You just

"Do I smell rodents?"

need to motivate her. One way is to walk a short distance alone dropping treats along the way. Then let her start on the trail and help her discover she can find treats by following your scent. As she catches on you can drop the treats farther apart, until eventually only the mother lode of treats remains at the end of the trail. If you have a helper, you can use yourself as the reward, so your Dachshund has to follow your trail for longer and longer distances to find you. This only works if she wants to find you, of course; some Dachshunds just take the opportunity to go for a walk without you.

With their long snouts and short legs, Dachshund noses are ideally situated for heavy-duty tracking. But minis may face some challenges when traversing long tracks over rough terrain. That's where the Dachshund fortitude takes over. Minis and standards alike have earned tracking titles.

The AKC Tracking Dog (TD) title is earned by following a 440- to 500-yard track with three to five turns laid by a person from 30 minutes to 2 hours before.

The Tracking Dog Excellent (TDX) title is earned by following an 800- to 1000-yard track with five to seven turns laid 3 to 5 hours earlier. The track crosses a fresher track laid by another person and may traverse various

The Dachshund's nose can detect one special scent amid a bouquet of other smells.

types of terrain and obstacles, including plowed land, woods, streams, bridges, and lightly traveled roads.

The Variable Surface Tracking (VST) title is earned by following a 3- to 5-hour track, 600 to 800 yards long, over a variety of surfaces such as might be normally encountered when tracking in the real world. At least three different surfaces, including one with vegetation and two without, must be included. Tracks may go through buildings and may be crossed by animal, pedestrian, or vehicular traffic.

The Champion Tracker (CT) title is earned by passing all three of the tracking tests (TD, TDX, and VST).

Dachshunds of Distinction
• The first TDX Dachshund was Gretel von Bupp Murr UDTX UD, in 1980. The UDTX signifies Gretel also had a UD title; in fact, Gretel earned UDTX titles in the United States, Canada, and Bermuda.
• The first VST and CT Dachshund was CT DC Sadsack The Cupid Clone MW ME, in 2002. Only one other Dachshund has obtained the coveted CT: CT FC Owl Farms Rising Star ML UD TDX AXJ MX ME.

Blood Trailing

What sounds somewhat grisly is in reality one of the most humane activities Dachshunds partake in. Blood trailing refers to tracking wounded animals, usually deer, with dogs so that they do not suffer a lingering death. In some European countries hunters are required to use dogs to find wounded game, but only a few states in America allow the use of dogs for this purpose.

Dachshunds have become the most popular breed for blood trailing. Their deliberate, slow way of working makes it easier to keep up with them and may be one reason they seem less likely to stray from the trail of blood. A blood trailer must stay with the scent of blood even though the trail is crossed by fresher deer scent. Many other breeds are too tempted and have a tendency to follow the fresher deer scent. Not the Dachshund. Beacuse Dachshunds are small, they are easy to transport and more adept at following trails into thickets, but their size can also render them more susceptible to cactus thorns and snakebites to the face. Blood-trailing dogs are worked on long leashes, and they are not to attack or corner the wounded animal. Wirehaired Dachshunds from European lines have traditionally been most successful at blood trailing. These dogs have slightly longer legs and often many generations of blood trailers behind them. However, Dachshunds from pure American lines have also proved themselves adept trailers.

In the United States, the most active group of blood trailers is Deer Search, based in New York. Founders of Deer Search were instrumental in legalizing the use of dogs to track wounded big game in New York, and they now promote this activity in other states as well. For more information contact them at *http://www.deersearch.org*. Deer Search sponsors blood-trailing tests and competitions in which dogs must track a 20- to 24-hour-old, 800- to 1000-meter blood trail having three 90-degree turns. Complete rules can be found at the Deer Search web site.

Blood-trailing tests are more popular in European countries, particularly

"Please take me tracking!"

Hot on the trail . . . (chocolate Smooth standard).

Field Trials

Dachshunds have been competing in AKC- or DCA-sanctioned field trials since the 1930s. They competed under existing beagle field trial rules until 1985, when they switched to more Dachshund-appropriate rules. Dachshund field trials are usually held in large fenced areas. A long line of people walk abreast until a rabbit is spotted. The *"Tally-Ho"* is shouted, and two Dachshunds (a brace) are brought to the spot where the rabbit was last seen and allowed to sniff around until they indicate they've found the scent. The dogs are held on long lines looped through their collars, so once the handler is sure the dog is on the trail, the line can be slipped through the collar and the dog set free to trail. The judges follow behind the dogs as they trail, evaluating their ability. The rabbit is never caught or killed. The dogs are instead judged in relation to one another on their prowess in picking up the trail, their persistence in following it, the degree to which they give tongue (or bay), and whether they flush the rabbit. Winners of each brace as well as other impressive dogs are called back for a second run, and eventually the judges place the dogs according to their performance. Dachshunds placing first through fourth in an Open All-Age stake earn from one-quarter (fourth place) to one point (first place) for every dog they defeat, which count toward the 35 points necessary to become a Field Champion.

Germany. The dogs follow a 1-kilometer trail of Roe deer blood through a forest riddled with distracting scent lines of deer and fox, sometimes on trails as old as 40 hours!

Dachshunds of Distinction
• FC Clary von Moosbach was the first Deer Search dog, a pioneer in America. She located more than 70 wounded deer. But she was also a talented rabbit hunter, and even did a good impersonation of a bird dog, finding and retrieving upland birds. At night she doubled as a coon dog, treeing raccoons.
• FC von Hohenwald Missy TD, ME is best known as a blood-trailing dog. Her 129 finds have earned her a spot in the Deer Search Hall of Fame. But in her spare time she also won the DCA National Field Trial three times, earned an AKC TD, and became a Master Earthdog.

Many canine field sports require hours of extensive training before a dog is ready to compete. While training helps, the Dachshund is such a natural hunter that even dogs that have never trailed have been known to make dazzling debuts in the field. And while having a pedigree filled with Field Champions (FCs) helps, some spectacular field Dachshunds come from show lines or no particular lines at all.

Training helps even the best Dachshund touch basis with her hunting roots, however. You can start by dragging a piece of canvas scented with rabbit scent (available at most hunting stores). Start with short, simple tracks and, when she finds the lure at the end, let her play tug of war or fetch with it. You can also go looking for real rabbits to trail in the field. You can train on a long line at first until you're sure your dog will come back. It's best to train only in fenced areas where you know of any hazards.

All field trials are special events, but the year's highlights are the Dachshund Club of America Annual Field Trial held in New Jersey, and the National Field Trial, usually held in conjunction with the DCA National

Dachshunds of Distinction
• The first Dachshund FC was Amsel v Holzgarten in 1936.
• The first Dachshund to be a Dual Champion (both conformation and field champion) was DC Uta von Moosbach.

Specialty show at a roving location throughout the country.

Field trials entail long days of tramping through all sorts of terrain in all sorts of weather. Be prepared with good hiking boots, all-weather gear, and water for your dog. And make sure both of you are in shape!

Earthdog Trials

No matter how domesticated your Dachshund is, her genes push her to dig and burrow and sniff out vermin. She may try to do this in your yard, your sofa, or under your house, but if she's lucky, you'll give her the chance to do it at an earthdog trial. These trials are designed to simulate the conditions a Dachshund or terrier might encounter in the field, requiring her to enter a tunnel and proceed down it and around corners until she finds a caged rat, which she should then "mark" by scratching, barking, whining, or digging for a sustained time period.

Chances are you won't happen to have a rat and a tunnel in your yard or even your neighborhood park. You'll need to make your own or find a trial that offers the AKC *Introduction to Quarry* class. This class allows novice dogs to experience the thrill of the hunt. Dogs need no training to participate. You release the dog 10 feet from the tunnel entrance and then stand quietly beside the entrance. The tunnel is 10 feet long with one 90-degree turn. The natural instincts of most Dachshunds propel them right into the tunnel until they come face to face with the first rodent many of them have ever seen. Many Dachshunds will instinctively bark and work the quarry, but others remain hesitant. With some encouragement from the judge most catch on quickly and subsequently have to be pulled from the tunnel under protest, still slinging threats at the rat that so rudely ignored them. Those dogs that reach the quarry within 2 minutes and work it for 30 seconds receive a passing score. However, as this class does not lead to a title, passing or failing is not the important factor here; leaving the trial with a dog itching to do it again is the real reward.

Some Dachshunds learn better at home, away from the excitement of a trial. If you're willing to dig up part of your yard and keep a pet rat, you

Dachshunds use all their senses when hunting.

may have the makings of an earthdog trainer. Place the rat in a small, secure cage. Make a big deal out of showing it to her, excitedly whispering "Rat!" while keeping it just out of her reach. Let her approach the cage on her own time and get a good sniff, and then gradually move the cage about. Once she's keen, hold her back from the cage so she really wants to get to it. The more frustrated she is, the more she will bark, and barking is essential for an earthdog. Reward barking by letting her have a quick bite at the cage and then restrain her again. Never allow her to touch the rat. Killing tame rats will not help her enthusiasm and is unfair and cruel. Most rats grow accustomed to the dogs barking, but they will never grow accustomed to physical abuse or neglect. Be as good a rat owner as you are a dog owner.

Introduction to Tunnels

You don't need a rat to get your Dachshund to go underground. You don't even need a real tunnel at first. Just use a couple of cardboard boxes and drag a fur toy on a string through them, enticing your dog to follow. Let her catch it and then have a good game of tug o' war while she's still in the box. When she's running through the makeshift box without hesitation, it's time to move to a better tunnel.

You should be able to buy a 5-foot section of drain pipe and secure it on top of the ground. If you can't find one, you can use straw bales to fashion tunnels in your yard, or you

"Nobody in here!"

can make your own tunnels (or liners, as they are called) using wood for the sides and top, keeping the natural earth floor. Start with the liners above ground, and use only a short, straight section. Then gradually add more distance and a turn or two. If your liner has a removable top you can run a string through the tunnel with a toy on it and lead your dog through it. The size of the tunnels in a trial are 9 by 9 inches; you can start a little larger and then work down toward the narrower size. If you really don't mind destroying your yard (and let's face it, your Dachshund has probably already done that for you), you can sink your liners into the ground so the tops are flush with ground level. But a warning: This

only works on high ground; otherwise the tunnels will be flooded with the first good rain. Note, too, that this may well be the final step in convincing your neighbors that you are more than a little odd.

If you have a caged rat, place it at the far end of the tunnel, tell your dog *"Rat!,"* and show her the rat through the tunnel opening. Use a barricade so she can't run around the tunnel to the rat. If she won't enter the tunnel, make the tunnel shorter. Stuffing her into it will only alarm her more. Once she's charging through the tunnel without hesitation, introduce a turn at the very beginning. The next training step is to spray animal scent, available at hunting stores, in a trail leading through the tunnel to the rat.

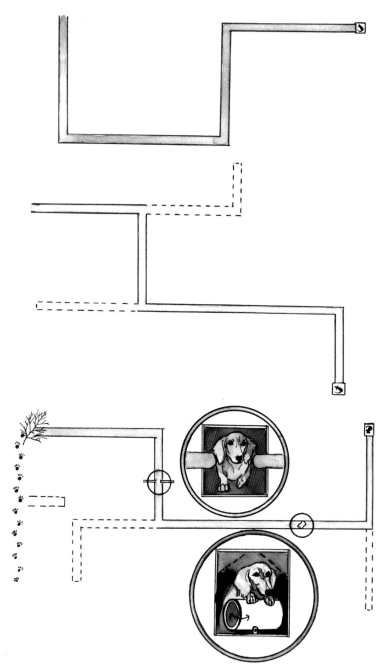

Earthdog tunnels (from top: Junior, Senior, and Master tunnels).

Eventually your dog will cue on the scent to find the tunnel entrance.

The AKC offers three increasingly challenging levels of earthdog testing after the *Introduction to Quarry*, leading to the Junior, Senior, and Master Earthdog titles.

In the *Junior Earthdog* test, the dog is released 10 feet from the tunnel entrance and has 30 seconds to traverse the 30-foot long tunnel with its three 90-degree turns and reach the quarry, which it must then work continuously for 1 minute. The dog must qualify twice to earn the Junior Earthdog title.

The *Senior Earthdog* test is more like a real hunting situation. The dog is released 20 feet from a steep, partially hidden entrance. The dog must use a scent trail to choose this correct entrance over a second, false entrance. The design of this tunnel is the same as that for the Junior test, with two tricky differences: a false exit that goes for about 7 feet and has one right angle turn, and a tunnel leading to a false den that contains bedding but no rat. The dog has 90 seconds to reach the real rat and must work it for another 90 seconds. Then the rat is blocked from the dog's view and removed, and the dog must retrace her path out to her handler when called. This simulates the field situation in which the quarry bolts from the den. A dog that refuses to leave the den when called is a serious liability in the field. Dachshunds that pass the Senior level test three times are crowned Senior Earthdogs and can now compete in an even more challenging test.

American Working Terrier Association

The American Working Terrier Association (AWTA) is the original sponsor of earthdog trials and welcomes Dachshunds at its trials. The concept is the same as in AKC earthdog trials. The AWTA offers the *Novice* class for beginners, in which the tunnel is 10 feet long with one right angle turn. The dog is released 10 feet away from the tunnel's entrance and has 1 minute to reach the quarry (2 minutes for half credit), which she must then work for 30 seconds. Dogs that pass at the Novice level move on to the next level, the Open/Certificate of Gameness class. The *Certificate of Gameness (CG)* is awarded to dogs that travel a 30-foot tunnel with three right-angle turns, reaching the quarry within 30 seconds and working it for another minute. In both cases the dog is given only one command from the handler upon release, with no subsequent urging or encouragement.

The *Master Earthdog* test adds more elements that would be found in a real hunting situation. Two dogs are released about 100 feet from the tunnel entrance, which is somewhat hidden and blocked with a removable obstruction. An unscented false tunnel is located along the scent line leading to the real tunnel. The dogs have 1 minute to locate the correct entrance, whereupon one dog is

Entering an Earthdog tunnel.

staked out while the other is allowed to enter the tunnel. Just as in a real underground den, the tunnel contains a couple of surprises: a constriction point where the tunnel narrows to only 6 inches wide, and an obstruction posed by a 6-inch-diameter pipe that can be moved by the dog 2½ inches. The dog has 90 seconds to reach the quarry and must work it for another 90 seconds, during which time tapping noises simulating the hunter digging to the quarry are made by the judge. Meanwhile the

staked (or honoring) dog should remain reasonably quiet; the two dogs will switch places once the first one is finished. A dog must qualify at four trials to add the prestigious Master Earthdog title to its name.

Hunting

The liveliest things most Dachshunds ever get to hunt are morsels dropped from your table, but even the most ardent chowhound would trade being under the table at a feast of klutzes for the chance to go hunting for food on the hoof—or at least a furry animal down a hole.

Dachshunds in European countries are more likely to be used for their native hunting purpose, but they adapt to native quarry around the world. They are one of dogdom's most versatile hunters, working in packs to follow wild boar, working alone or in pairs on the trail of rabbits, or going underground to face a badger or woodchuck one on one.

Rabbits are probably the most popular quarry, in part because they're the most widespread. Dachshunds of all sizes can flush a rabbit ensconced in a thicket or trail it through rough terrain. Some will bay while others will remain quiet on the trail. Since the thrill is in the hunt, you need not shoot the rabbit once you've located it, as long as you let your dog know she is a great hunter.

In areas in which woodchucks (also know as groundhogs) dig dens, Dachshunds are sometimes used to

Dachshunds of Distinction

In 1996 FC BeeJays Chocolate Smoke CD TD ME became the first dog of any breed to earn the Master Earthdog title. Four of the first five Master Earthdogs were Dachshunds.

locate an occupied den and either bolt the animal from its den or go in after it. Be forewarned that unlike rabbit hunting, it is more difficult to spare the life of a woodchuck once a Dachshund goes after it unless your dog is trained well enough that she will leave her quarry underground. Experienced Dachshunds can also bolt, corner, or even take on foxes.

If you have squirrels in your yard, no doubt your Dachshund has already become proficient at treeing them, perhaps barking to tell you of their location. Squirrel hunting trials judge dogs of all breeds on their ability to do just that. Nocturnal Dachshunds can also trail and tree raccoons and opossums.

A few Dachshunds have even proven themselves in the world of bird hunting, flushing pheasants, grouse, and other upland game birds. They will gladly retrieve them, and some have even retrieved waterfowl.

Dachshunds are sometimes used together with falcons to hunt squirrels, rabbits, and birds. By flushing game birds into the air, keeping rabbits in open cover, or keeping squirrels high in the branches, Dachshunds give falcons a better opportunity of catching their quarry.

The North American Teckel Club was formed in 2000 to promote the use of Dachshunds for hunting in America. The game and terrain are different from those in Europe, but the Dachshunds don't mind. They offer tests based upon the European usefulness tests that encompass following blood trails, flushing rabbits,

Underground Precautions

Any time your dog may end up underground she should wear a remote locator collar. This collar emits a radio signal that is picked up by a handheld receiver, which the operator uses to locate the position of the dog. Before these collars the only way to find a dog underground was through careful listening—still a handy skill to have in the field. If your Dachshund is lost while she's not wearing a collar, and you suspect she could be stuck in a hole, look for burrows with evidence of digging or entry. If possible, use another dog with hunting experience, which will often go to the same hole (just don't let this dog out of your sight). Walk very quietly and listen for rustling or barking. Calling your dog seldom helps because most dogs will stop barking so they can listen—meaning you can walk right past your listening dog. When you find a likely hole, dig very carefully. A collapsed hole can fill the entrance with dirt, suffocating the entombed dog below.

locating and trailing small game, and locating and either bolting or baying underground quarry. Your Dachshund must be certified to be capable of participating in these events ahead of time.

The American Working Terrier Association issues the *Working Certificate (WC)* to Dachshunds that perform successfully in natural terrain with fox, badger, woodchuck, raccoon, or aggressive opossum. For obvious reasons, skunks are not acceptable! To do this, a dog must enter a natural earth den and locate quarry on its own; having found it, she must mark it (by barking or otherwise alerting the hunter) and either bolt it (flush it from the den), draw it (pull it from the den), or stay with it until the hunter digs it out. This must be accomplished in front of an AWTA member. The AWTA also awards the *Hunting Certificate (HC)* to Dachshunds regularly used for hunting game such as rabbits, squirrels, opossums, rats, raccoons, and muskrats or even for flushing and/or retrieving upland birds over a full hunting season.

If you are interested in hunting with your Dachshund, it's best to find an experienced hunting Dachshund person who can show you the ins and outs of local hunting areas and help ensure the safety of your dog. Find out about your local laws and hunting seasons; in many areas it is illegal to hunt mammals with dogs at any time. Hunting is serious business, and not something to be undertaken on a whim. Your dog must be in top shape with good muscle tone and the ability to keep up a good day's work. Every region of the country has its own particular dangers from animals, plants, land features, man-made dangers such as poisons, traps, and automobiles, and other hunters. Know them before venturing out into the wilds. Ask your veterinarian about any special vaccination precautions. Your hunting backpack should include a first aid kit, flashlight, towels, dog food, water, a metal dowel, an assortment of digging tools, and extra batteries for your remote collar.

Skunked!

If a skunk sprays your dog, take her to open air immediately and wash as much of the spray off her body as possible. Commercially available products such as Skunk Off! are handy for carrying in the field. At home, mix up a quart of 3 percent hydrogen peroxide, ¼ cup of baking soda, and 1 teaspoon of liquid soap. Use it immediately, sponging it all over your dog. Rinse off after about 5 minutes. If you wish to repeat it, mix up a new batch since it loses its ability to oxidize the offending chemicals (mercaptans) in skunk spray quickly. Other home remedies, such as tomato juice, can help by stripping away some of the oil base, but they don't neutralize the mercaptans remaining.

Chapter Ten

Built to Order

Long on looks and short on leg, the Dachshund's design is no accident. No other breed could do the jobs the Dachshund does, because no other breed is built like a Dachshund.

Bred for generations according to their hunting and working ability, today's Dachshunds are the result of the best bred to the best, tested by the best: the testing ground of real-life fieldwork. Few Dachshunds today have the chance to compete in the field, but it's vital that the traits the early breeders worked so diligently to set in the breed not be lost. If form defines function, then the potential for function should be evident by examining form. That's where the breed standard comes in.

You may think of your Dachshund as a house pet, but the standard emphasizes that the Dachshund is built to hunt. His short legs allow him to maneuver in tight spaces and his long body and developed musculature give him the power to face off against a formidable foe. The pliable skin gives him some wiggle room should his adversary get its teeth on him. He should never appear crippled,

and should be confident and alert. The design of the head, jaws, and teeth gives the Dachshund a strong and reaching grip. The neck is designed for maximum strength along with reach. The Dachshund's front assembly and prominent breastbone are hallmarks of the breed. Not only does the front assembly bear most of the dog's weight, but the Dachshund's front is also modified to allow it to dig and move in close quarters. Strong, durable feet are well arched and neither splayed nor flat. Knuckling over, in which the wrist joint flexes forward so it's in front of the pastern,

Dachshunds even retrieve!

creates a potentially crippling front assembly and is considered such a severe fault that dogs with it are disqualified and cannot be shown. The hindquarters provide the thrust and power to propel the Dachshund both above ground and below.

The AKC Dachshund Standard

General Appearance

Low to ground, long in body and short of leg with robust muscular development, the skin is elastic and pliable without excessive wrinkling. Appearing neither crippled, awkward, nor cramped in his capacity for movement, the Dachshund is well-balanced with bold and confident head carriage and intelligent, alert facial expression. His hunting spirit, good nose, loud tongue and distinctive build make him well-suited for below-ground work and for beating the bush. His keen nose gives him an advantage over most other breeds for trailing.

Note. Inasmuch as the Dachshund is a hunting dog, scars from honorable wounds shall not be considered a fault.

Size, Proportion, Substance

Bred and shown in two sizes, standard and miniature, miniatures are not a separate classification but compete in a class division for "11 pounds and under at 12 months of age and older." Weight of the standard size is usually between 16 and 32 pounds.

Head

Viewed from above or from the side, the head tapers uniformly to the tip of the nose. The eyes are of medium size, almond-shaped and

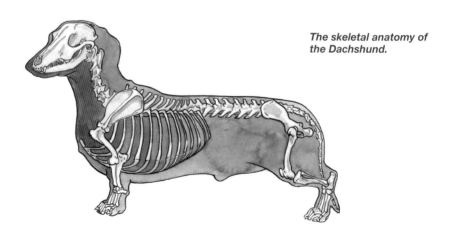

The skeletal anatomy of the Dachshund.

106

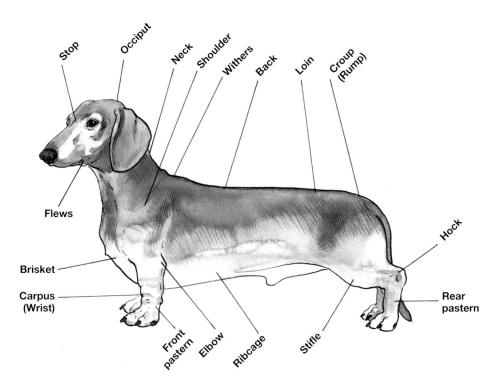

The external anatomy of the Dachshund.

dark-rimmed, with an energetic, pleasant expression; not piercing; very dark in color. The bridge bones over the eyes are strongly prominent. Wall eyes, except in the case of dappled dogs, are a serious fault. The ears are set near the top of the head, not too far forward, of moderate length, rounded, not narrow, pointed, or folded. Their carriage, when animated, is with the forward edge just touching the cheek so that the ears frame the face. The skull is slightly arched, neither too broad nor too narrow, and slopes gradually with little perceptible stop into the finely formed, slightly arched muzzle. Black is the preferred color of the nose. Lips are tightly stretched, well covering the lower jaw. Nostrils well open. Jaws opening wide and hinged well back of the eyes, with strongly developed bones and teeth. *Teeth*—Powerful canine teeth; teeth fit closely together in a scissors bite. An even bite is a minor fault. Any other deviation is a serious fault.

Neck

Long, muscular, clean-cut, without dewlap, slightly arched in the nape, flowing gracefully into the shoulders.

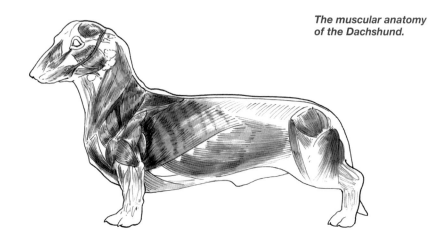

Trunk

The trunk is long and fully muscled. When viewed in profile, the back lies in the straightest possible line between the withers and the short very slightly arched loin. A body that hangs loosely between the shoulders is a serious fault. *Abdomen*—Slightly drawn up.

Forequarters

For effective underground work, the front must be strong, deep, long and cleanly muscled. Forequarters in detail: *Chest*—The breastbone is strongly prominent in front so that on either side a depression or dimple appears. When viewed from the front, the thorax appears oval and extends downward to the mid-point of the forearm. The enclosing structure of well-sprung ribs appears full and oval to allow, by its ample capacity, complete development of heart and lungs. The keel merges gradually into the line of the abdomen and extends well beyond the front legs. Viewed in profile, the lowest point of the breast line is covered by the front leg. *Shoulder Blades*—Long, broad, well-laid back and firmly placed upon the fully developed thorax, closely fitted at the withers, furnished with hard yet pliable muscles. *Upper Arm*—Ideally the same length as the shoulder blade and at right angles to the latter, strong of bone and hard of muscle, lying close to the ribs, with elbows close to the body, yet capable of free movement. *Forearm*—Short; supplied with hard yet pliable muscles on the front and outside, with tightly stretched tendons on the inside and at the back, slightly curved inwards. The joints between the forearms and the feet (wrists) are closer together than the shoulder joints, so that the front does not appear absolutely straight. Knuckling over is a disqualifying fault. *Feet*—Front paws are full, tight, compact, with well-arched toes and tough, thick pads. They may be equally inclined a trifle outward. There are five toes, four in use, close together with a pronounced arch and strong, short nails. Front dewclaws may be removed.

Hindquarters

Strong and cleanly muscled. The pelvis, the thigh, the second thigh, and the metatarsus are ideally the same length and form a series of right angles. From the rear, the thighs are strong and powerful. The legs turn neither in nor out. *Metatarsus*—Short and strong, perpendicular to the second thigh bone. When viewed from behind, they are upright and parallel. *Feet—Hind Paws*—Smaller than the front paws with four compactly closed and arched toes with tough, thick pads. The entire foot points straight ahead and is balanced equally on the ball and not merely on the toes. Rear dewclaws should be removed. *Croup*—Long, rounded and full, sinking *slightly* toward the tail. *Tail*—Set in continuation of the spine, extending without kinks, twists, or pronounced curvature, and not carried too gaily.

Gait

Fluid and smooth. Forelegs reach well forward, without much lift, in unison with the driving action of hind legs. The correct shoulder assembly and well-fitted elbows allow the long, free stride in front. Viewed from the front, the legs do not move in exact parallel planes, but incline slightly inward to compensate for shortness of leg and width of chest. Hind legs drive on a line with the forelegs, with

". . . clever, lively, and courageous to the point of rashness . . ."

hocks (metatarsus) turning neither in nor out. The propulsion of the hind leg depends on the dog's ability to carry the hind leg to complete extension. Viewed in profile, the forward reach of the hind leg equals the rear extension. The thrust of correct movement is seen when the rear pads are clearly exposed during rear extension. Feet must travel parallel to the line of motion with no tendency to swing out, cross over, or interfere with each other. Short, choppy movement, rolling or high-stepping gait, close or overly wide coming or going are incorrect. The Dachshund must have agility, freedom of movement, and endurance to do the work for which he was developed.

Temperament

The Dachshund is clever, lively and courageous to the point of rashness,

The Smooth Dachshund's coat is short, smooth, and shining.

persevering in above and below ground work, with all the senses well-developed. Any display of shyness is a serious fault.

Special Characteristics of the Three Coat Varieties

The Dachshund is bred with three varieties of coat: (1) Smooth; (2) Wirehaired; (3) Longhaired and is shown in two sizes, standard and miniature. All three varieties and both sizes must conform to the characteristics already specified. The following features are applicable for each variety.

Smooth Dachshund. *Coat*—Short, smooth and shining. Should be neither too long nor too thick. Ears not leathery. *Tail*—Gradually tapered to a point, well but not too richly haired. Long sleek bristles on the underside are considered a patch of strong-growing hair, not a fault. A brush tail is a fault, as is also a partly or wholly hairless tail.

Color of Hair—Although base color is immaterial, certain patterns and basic colors predominate. One-colored Dachshunds include red (with or without a shading of interspersed dark hairs or sable) and cream. A small amount of white on the chest is acceptable, but not desirable. Nose and nails—black.

Two-colored Dachshunds include black, chocolate, wild boar, gray (blue) and fawn (Isabella), each with tan markings over the eyes, on the sides of the jaw and underlip, on the inner edge of the ear, front, breast, inside and behind the front legs, on the paws and around the anus, and from there to about one-third to one-half of the length of the tail on the underside. Undue prominence or extreme lightness of tan markings is undesirable. A small amount of white on the chest is acceptable but not desirable. Nose and nails—in the case of black dogs, black; for chocolate and all other colors, dark brown, but self-colored is acceptable.

Dappled Dachshunds—The "single" dapple pattern is expressed as lighter-colored areas contrasting with the darker base color, which may be any acceptable color. Neither the light nor the dark color should predominate. Nose and nails are the same as for one and two-colored Dachshunds. Partial or wholly blue (wall) eyes are as acceptable as dark eyes. A large area of white on the chest of a dapple is permissible.

"Low to ground, long in body and short of leg with robust muscular development . . ."

A "double" dapple is one in which varying amounts of white coloring occur over the body in addition to the dapple pattern. Nose and nails: as for one and two-color Dachshunds; partial or wholly self-colored is permissible.

Brindle is a pattern (as opposed to a color) in which black or dark stripes occur over the entire body although in some specimens the pattern may be visible only in the tan points.

Wirehaired Dachshund. *Coat—* With the exception of jaw, eyebrows, and ears, the whole body is covered with a uniform tight, short, thick, rough, hard, outer coat but with finer, somewhat softer, shorter hairs (undercoat) everywhere distributed between the coarser hairs. The absence of an undercoat is a fault.

The distinctive facial furnishings include a beard and eyebrows. On the ears the hair is shorter than on the body, almost smooth. The general arrangement of the hair is such that the Wirehaired Dachshund, when viewed from a distance, resembles the smooth. *Any sort of soft hair in the outer coat, wherever found on the body, especially on the top of the head, is a fault.* The same is true of long, curly, or wavy hair, or hair that sticks out irregularly in all directions. *Tail—*Robust, thickly haired, gradually tapering to a point. A flag tail is a fault. *Color of Hair—* While the most common colors are wild boar, black and tan, and various shades of red, all colors are admissible. A small amount of white on the chest, although acceptable, is not

"For effective underground work, the front must be strong, deep, long and cleanly muscled."

desirable. Nose and nails—same as for the smooth variety.

Longhaired Dachshund. *Coat*— The sleek, glistening, often slightly wavy hair is longer under the neck and on the forechest, the underside of the body, the ears, and behind the legs. The coat gives the dog an elegant appearance. Short hair on the ear is not desirable. Too profuse a coat which masks type, equally long hair over the whole body, a curly coat, or a pronounced parting on the back are faults. *Tail*—Carried gracefully in prolongation of the spine; the hair attains its greatest length here and forms a veritable flag.

Color of Hair—Same as for the Smooth Dachshund. Nose and nails— same as for the smooth.

The foregoing description is that of the ideal Dachshund. Any deviation from the above described dog must be penalized to the extent of the deviation keeping in mind the importance of the contribution of the various features toward the basic original purpose of the breed.

Disqualification
Knuckling over of front

Approved April 7, 1992
Effective May 27, 1992

Conformation Shows

Conformation shows compare each dog to the breed standard, evaluating type, soundness, temperament, coat, and adding a little extra for showmanship. Type refers to the extent that a Dachshund is a Dachshund: "Low to the ground, long in body and short of leg with robust muscular development." The standard goes on to describe essential aspects of the head, expression, and other subtle points that are essential to good Dachshund type. Soundness refers to a dog's ability to do the work for which it was bred. To do so a dog must have proper body structure and move efficiently. The standard describes proper movement in part as "fluid and smooth." Temperament refers to the proper temperament for the breed: "clever, lively and courageous to the point of rashness."

The Dachshund standard is among the more exacting of dog breed standards, and is the blueprint by which Dachshund judges make their decisions. Your first step as a potential conformation exhibitor is to study the standard, study successful conformation Dachshunds, and study your own dog. No dog is perfect, but as long as your dog is neither neutered nor spayed, has two normally descended testicles (if male), does not knuckle over in the front legs (a Dachshund-specific disqualification), and will not bite the judge, he can be shown.

If you can find a handling class you're in luck, but if not, you can still practice at home. At a dog show your Dachshund will need to pose for the judge both on the floor and on an exam table. Study photos of Dachshunds being shown: the topline level, the tail straight out behind, the head up, front legs roughly parallel with the feet allowed to point slightly outward, hind legs parallel with the line from hock to feet. He must be able to hold this pose while the judge looks in his mouth to evaluate his bite, feels his body all over to evaluate his conformation, and even checks to make sure those testicles are present. You convince your dog to do all this by rewarding him with treats for standing longer and longer periods.

Your Dachshund will also need to know how to trot alongside you without planting his butt, playing whirling dervish, galloping, zigzagging, or scavenging for dropped food—a mighty temptation when you're already so close to the ground! Practice by striding decisively toward a goal, giving your dog a treat when

you get there. As impossible as it may seem, every perfectly behaved Dachshund you see on the television coverage of Westminster once started as a dog that did everything yours is doing!

At AKC shows, Dachshunds compete against others of their coat type, in one of several classes divided by age and other factors. All the class winners within a coat type of one sex then compete against each other for Winners Dog or Winners Bitch, with the winner earning up to 5 points toward the 15 points needed for its championship according to how many dogs it defeats. This dog then competes against the Dachshunds that are already champions for the awards of Best of Variety (BOV), Best of Opposite Sex to the dog that wins BOV, and Best of Winners (either the Winners Dog or Winners Bitch). Only at specialty shows, which are

An Isabella-colored puppy.

The body coat of the Wirehaired Dachshund is tight, short, thick, rough, and hard, with somewhat shorter and softer hairs distributed between the coarser hairs.

group winners for Best in Show. Here the Dachshund meets even tougher competition, but many Dachshunds have emerged at the end of the show as the only undefeated dog of the day: the Best in Show winner!

Most Dachshunds fanciers spend an entire lifetime without winning a Best in Show; in fact, only a minority win groups. They know that winning is fun, but the real fun of dog shows lies in spending a special day with your dog, socializing with other Dachshund fanciers, and watching the other dogs. Only one dog can leave the show undefeated, but every dog can leave the show a winner as long as they keep dog shows in perspective. Don't let the color of your dog's ribbons color your perception of him; he already knows he's the best dog there!

prestigious shows just for Dachshunds, do the winners of the three varieties compete for best Dachshund, or Best of Breed, at AKC shows. Instead, at all-breed shows each of the three BOV winners then goes on to compete in the hound group. The United Kennel Club divides the breed into Standard and Miniature varieties. In some countries, such as Canada, Dachshunds are divided by both size and coat, so they send six representatives to the hound group. Several European countries devote an entire group exclusively to Dachshunds.

Dachshunds may be the smallest members of the hound group, but they loom large in winning statistics. They are extremely competitive, often winning first in group. Having won the hound group, the winner then competes against the other six

For the Record
• The first AKC Champion Dachshund was Ch. Dash in 1885.
• The first miniature Dachshund to become a champion was the Wirehaired Ch. Limelight Berlinerlicht in 1941.
• The first Dachshund to win an AKC Best in Show was International Ch. Kensal Call Boy.
• Several Dachshunds have won the Hound Group at the prestigious Westminster Kennel Club, most recently the Longhaired Ch. Dramada's Curmudgeon in 1998 and the year before that the Wirehaired Ch. Starbarrack Malachite SW.

Chapter Eleven

The Dachshund Doctor

Most popular breeds are beset with health problems. Not the Dachshund. But Dachshunds still have some hereditary heartaches and the regular assortment of everyday illnesses. Walking the fine line between negligent and hypochondriac owner is tough, even for experienced Dachshund owners. Knowing the signs of good health will give you a head start.

Signs of a Healthy Dachshund

Understanding the normal values for your dog will help you detect when something isn't right.

Gum Color

One simple guide to your dog's health is his gum color. Check it especially if your dog appears weak or lethargic.
• Normal gum color is a good deep pink.
• Pale or especially whitish gum color can indicate shock, anemia, or poor circulation.
• Bluish gum or tongue color indicates imminent life-threatening lack of oxygen.

• Bright red gum color can indicate carbon monoxide poisoning.
• Yellowish color can indicate jaundice.
• Little tiny red splotches (called petechia) can indicate a blood-clotting problem.

Don't confuse a red line around the gum line with healthy gums. A dog with dirty teeth can have gum disease, giving an unhealthy, but rosy, glow to the gums, especially at the margins around the teeth.

Besides color, capillary refill time, which is an index of blood circulation, can be estimated simply by pressing on the gum with your finger and lifting your finger off. The gum where you pressed will be white momentarily, but will quickly re-pink as the blood moves back into the area. If it takes longer than a couple of seconds to re-pink, circulation is poor.

Body Temperature

Your Dachshund's body temperature is another clue about what's going on inside. As in humans, temperature will be slightly lower in the morning and higher in the evening. Normal temperature for a Dachshund is about 101 to 102°F. If the temperature is

• 103°F or above, call the veterinarian and ask for advice.
• 105°F or above, go to the veterinarian. A temperature of 106°F and above is dangerous.
• 98°F or below, call the veterinarian and ask for advice. Meanwhile cover the dog and try to warm her.
• 96°F or below, go to the veterinarian. Treat for hypothermia on the way.

Pulse

The easiest way to check your dog's pulse is to feel the pulse through the femoral artery. If your dog is standing, cup your hand around the top of her leg and feel around the inside of it, almost where it joins with the torso. If your dog is on her back, you can sometimes even see the pulse in this area. Normal pulse rate

A dog's temperature is an important sign of its general well-being.

for a Dachshund at rest is about 70 to 120 beats per minute.

You can feel your dog's heart beat by placing your hand on her lower ribcage just behind the elbow. Don't be alarmed if it seems irregular; the heartbeat of many dogs is irregular compared to humans. Have your veterinarian check it out, then get used to how it feels when it is normal.

Hydration

Repeated vomiting, diarrhea, or overheating can quickly lead to dehydration. To check your dog's hydration pick up the skin on the back just above the shoulders, so that it makes a slight tent above the body. It should snap back into place almost immediately. If it remains tented and separated from the body, your dog is dehydrated. You can also touch your dog's gums; if they are tacky rather than slick she may be dehydrated. The most obvious treatment is to give her some water. If she's dehydrated from vomiting or diarrhea, she may need intravenous or subcutaneous fluids.

Blood Tests

Your Dachshund's blood can provide valuable clues about her health. The most common tests are the Complete Blood Count (CBC) and the Serum Chemistry Profile ("Chem panel"). Many other specialized tests are fairly common.

CBC reports:
• Red blood cells: the cells responsible for carrying oxygen throughout the body

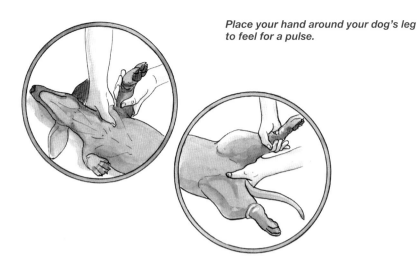

Place your hand around your dog's leg to feel for a pulse.

• White blood cells: the infection-fighting cells

• Platelets: components responsible for clotting blood to stop bleeding

Serum Chemistry Profile reports:

• Albumin (ALB): reduced levels are suggestive of liver or kidney disease, or parasites

• Alanine aminotransferase (ALT): elevated levels suggest liver disease

• Alkaline phosphatase (ALKP): elevated levels can indicate liver disease or Cushing's syndrome

• Amylase (AMYL): elevated levels suggest pancreatic or kidney disease

• Blood urea nitrogen (BUN): elevated levels suggest kidney disease

• Calcium (CA): elevated levels suggest kidney or parathyroid disease or some types of tumors

• Cholesterol (CHOL): elevated levels suggest liver or kidney disease or several other disorders

• Creatinine (CREA): elevated levels suggest kidney disease or urinary obstruction

• Blood Glucose (GLU): low levels can suggest liver disease

• Phosphorous (PHOS): elevated levels can suggest kidney disease

• Total bilirubin (TBIL): level can indicate problems in the bile ducts

• Total protein (TP): level can indicate problems of the liver, kidney, or gastrointestinal tract

The Five-Minute Checkup

The best 5 minutes you can spend with your dog every week is performing a quick health check. You'll be getting to know how your dog looks when she's healthy, you'll get a head start on any problems, and your dog will think you just can't resist petting her all over.

Check the

• Mouth for red, bleeding, swollen or pale gums, loose teeth, ulcers of the tongue or gums, or bad breath

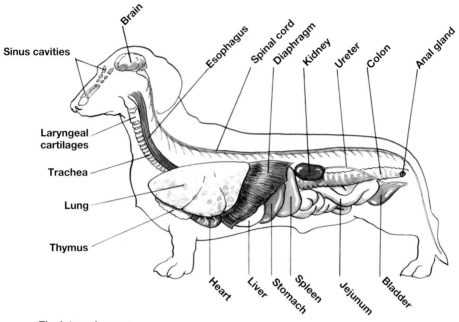

The internal organs.

Brain

Sinus cavities

Esophagus

Spinal cord

Diaphragm

Kidney

Ureter

Colon

Anal gland

Laryngeal cartilages

Trachea

Lung

Thymus

Heart

Liver

Stomach

Spleen

Jejunum

Bladder

• Eyes for discharge, cloudiness, or discolored "whites"
• Ears for foul odor, redness, discharge, or crusted tips
• Nose for thickened or colored discharge
• Skin for parasites, hair loss, crusts, red spots, or lumps
• Feet for cuts, abrasions, split nails, bumps, or misaligned toes
• Anal region for redness, swelling, discharge, or tracts

Watch your dog for signs of lameness or incoordination, sore neck, circling, loss of muscling, and any other behavioral change. Run your hands over the muscles and bones and check that they are symmetrical from one side to the other. Weigh your dog to see if she is gaining or losing. Check for growths, swellings sores, pigmented lumps, mammary masses, changes in testicle size, discharge from the vulva or penis, increased or decreased urination, foul smelling or strangely colored urine, incontinence, swollen abdomen, black or bloody stool, change in appetite or water consumption, difficulty breathing, lethargy, coughing, gagging, or loss of balance.

Behavior Changes

When a normally active, impetuous Dachshund suddenly slows down for no apparent reason, it's

time to investigate. Lethargy is the most common behavioral sign of disease. Possible causes could include
• Infection (check for fever)
• Anemia (check gum color)
• Circulatory problem (check gum color and pulse)
• Pain (check limbs, neck, and vertebrae for paralysis or signs of discomfort upon movement; check mouth, ears, and eyes for signs of pain; check abdomen for pain—pain in the abdomen often causes dogs to stand in a hunched position)
• Sudden loss of vision
• Poisoning (check gum color and pupil reaction, look for signs of vomiting or abdominal pain)
• Cancer
• Metabolic diseases
• Hypoglycemia (see page 39)

Unprecedented behavior of any kind, but particularly persistent circling or pacing, disorientation, loss of balance, head-pressing, hiding, tremors, seizures, lack of bowel or urine control, or a dramatic change in appetite are usually signs of a physical problem and need to be checked by your veterinarian.

Sick dogs often lie quietly in a curled or hunched up position. Dogs with abdominal pain often stand in "the position of relief," a bowing position with the front down and rear up. They also tend to walk around or dig at the ground. Shivering can also be a sign of pain. Dogs with breathing difficulties often refuse to lie down, or if they do, they lie on the chest and point the muzzle upward in order to breathe better.

Common Signs of Illness

Diarrhea

Diarrhea can result from overexcitement or nervousness, a change in diet or water, sensitivity to certain foods, overeating, intestinal parasites, viral or bacterial infections, or ingestion of toxic substances. Bloody diarrhea, diarrhea with vomiting, fever, or other signs of toxicity, or a diarrhea that lasts for more than a day should not be allowed to continue without veterinary advice.

Less severe diarrhea can be treated at home by withholding or severely restricting food and water for 24 hours (assuming no other medical problems exist that don't allow that). Administer human diarrhea medication in the same weight dosage as recommended for humans. A bland diet consisting of

Dachshunds are tough and may not always show signs of illness; the wise owner learns to recognize them.

Dachshund Health Concerns

• Several eye problems are encountered in Dachshunds. Microphthalmia is a condition in which the globe of the eye is abnormally small. The eye may still be functional, but is more likely to develop cataracts or a detached retina. Microphthalmia is seen more often in double dapples. Glaucoma and progressive retinal atrophy (PRA), both usually blinding, have been reported in the breed. Chorioretinal dysplasia, which also causes visual deficits, is occasionally seen. Keratoconjunctivitis sicca and pannus are problematic conditions of the cornea seen more commonly in Dachshunds. Entropion, a condition in which the lid is inverted so that it irritates the eye, is seen. Blindness associated with double dapples is not uncommon.

• Skin problems include color dilution alopecia (hair loss associated with blue coat coloration), pattern baldness (early hair loss starting in puppyhood), demodectic mange (a potentially devastating parasitic skin disease that can be difficult to cure), panniculitis (painful inflammation of subcutaneous fat layer), pemphigus (autoimmune problems causing ulceration of the skin), and, rarely, cutaneous asthenia (extreme skin fragility).

• Skeletal problems include the breed's biggest problem, intervertebral disk disease. Dachshunds with calcified disks, as seen on radiographs, are at greater risk of developing problems, and are also more likely to produce puppies with problems. Occasionally seen is ununited anconeal process, a type of elbow dysplasia causing lameness. Some dogs have a severe overbite, referred to as a parrot mouth (technically brachgnathism). This is often associated with a comparatively narrow lower jaw, which can cause the lower canines to jab into the roof of the mouth.

• Urinary system problems include renal hypoplasia, in which underdeveloped kidneys eventually result in kidney failure if untreated, and urinary stones of the bladder.

• Dachshunds have an increased tendency to be diabetic.

• Epilepsy can occur in any breed of dog, but there appears to be a genetic basis for it in at least some Dachshunds.

• Dachshunds have an increased incidence of Cushing's disease (hyperadrenocorticism) compared to other breeds.

• Von Willebrand's disease, a clotting defect leading to prolonged bleeding, is seen occasionally.

• Cryptorchidism, in which one or both testicles fail to descend into the scrotum, occurs especially in miniature Dachshunds.

• Dachshunds have a tendency to become overweight and even obese.

rice, tapioca, or cooked macaroni, along with cottage cheese or tofu for protein, should be given for several days. The intestinal tract needs time off in order to heal.

Vomiting

Vomiting may or may not indicate a serious problem. Vomiting after eating grass is common and usually of no great concern. Overeating is a common cause of occasional vomiting in puppies, especially if they follow eating with playing. Regurgitation immediately after meals could indicate a problem of the esophagus. Repeated vomiting could indicate that the dog has eaten spoiled food or indigestible objects or may have stomach illness. Veterinary advice should be sought. Meanwhile withhold food (or feed as directed for diarrhea) and restrict water.

Consult your veterinarian immediately if your dog vomits a foul substance resembling fecal matter (indicating a blockage in the intestinal tract) or blood (partially digested blood resembles coffee grounds), has accompanying fever or pain, or if there is projectile or continued vomiting. Sporadic vomiting with poor appetite and generally poor condition could indicate internal parasites or a more serious internal disease that should also be checked by your veterinarian.

Coughing

Allergies, foreign bodies, pneumonia, parasites, tracheal collapse, tumors, kennel cough, and heart dis-

Your Dachshund's health is the product of good genes, good care, and good luck.

ease can all cause coughing. Any cough lasting longer than a few days or accompanied by weakness or difficulty breathing warrants a veterinary consultation. Coughing irritates the throat and can lead to secondary infections if allowed to continue unchecked. It can also be miserable for the dog.

Kennel cough is a highly communicable airborne disease caused by several different infectious agents (but most often by Bordetella). It is characterized by a gagging cough arising about a week after exposure. Inoculations are available and may be advisable for dogs that are around strange dogs.

Congestive heart failure can cause coughing, most often following exercise or at night. Affected dogs will often lie down and point their nose in the air in order to breathe better. Drug and diet therapy can help affected dogs breathe better.

Lethargy can be a sign of illness.

Abnormal Urination

If your Dachshund has difficulty or pain when urinating, urinates suddenly and often but in small amounts, or passes cloudy or bloody urine, he may be suffering from a problem of the bladder, urethra, or prostate. Dribbling of urine during sleep can indicate a hormonal problem and is most common in spayed females. Urinalysis and a rectal exam by your veterinarian are necessary to diagnose the exact nature of the problem. Bladder infections must be treated promptly to prevent the infection from reaching the kidneys.

Blockage of urine can result in death. Inability to urinate requires immediate emergency veterinary attention.

Kidney disease, ultimately leading to kidney failure, is one of the most common ailments of older dogs. Young Dachshunds may also suffer from renal hypoplasia, leading to kidney failure at a young age. The earliest symptom is usually increased drinking and urination. Although the excessive urination may cause problems in keeping your house clean or your night's sleep intact, never try to restrict water from a dog with kidney disease. The fluid is necessary to flush out toxins that the kidneys are failing to flush with normal fluid levels. Feeding a diet low in foods that create these toxic by-products (that is, a diet with medium levels of high-quality protein to cut down on nitrogen and phosphorus) and administering fluids can help make a dog with kidney failure feel better.

Increased urination can also be a sign of diabetes or a urinary tract infection. Urine tests can usually diagnose the problem. Dachshunds are prone to urinary stones, particularly struvite, cystine, and calcium oxalate stones, all of which can cause painful urination and bloody urine. Surgical removal or dissolution is the treatment of choice, although sometimes they can be controlled through special diets.

Diabetes mellitus is signaled by excessive drinking and urination. Controlling the disease usually involves controlling the diet and administering insulin injections.

In males, infections of the *prostate gland* can lead to repeated urinary tract infections, and sometimes painful defecation or blood and pus in the urine. Castration and long-term antibiotic therapy is usually required for improvement.

Anal Discomfort

Licking of the anus or scooting of the rear along the ground can indicate recent diarrhea, but may also signal anal sac impaction. Dogs have two anal sacs that are normally emptied by rectal pressure during defecation or forcibly ejected when a dog is extremely frightened. Sometimes they fail to empty properly and become impacted or infected. Impacted sacs hurt and can swell so much they rupture through the dog's skin. Treatment consists of manually emptying the sacs, sometimes refilling them with an antibiotic ointment and giving the dog oral antibiotics.

Eye Problems

Squinting or tearing can be due to an irritated cornea or foreign body. Examine under the lids and flood the eye with saline solution, or use a moist cotton swab to remove any debris. If no improvement is seen after a day, have your veterinarian take a look. A watery discharge without squinting can be a symptom of allergies or a tear drainage problem. A clogged tear drainage duct can cause the tears to drain onto the face rather than the normal drainage through the nose. Your veterinarian can diagnose a drainage problem with a simple test.

Microphthalmia is a condition in which the globe of the eye is abnormally small. At some point the small size affects vision and the dog has poor or no vision. The condition is more common in double dapples. No treatment is available.

Keratoconjunctivitis sicca (KCS, or dry eye) is a potentially blinding condition that too often goes untreated. Tears are vital for the health of the cornea (the clear outer layer of the eye). When tears are absent or reduced, the cornea dries out, becomes dull looking, and eventually may become inflamed, infected, ulcerated, and opaque. It's an uncomfortable condition, and the eye will often have mucous discharge. KCS is more common in older dogs. Your veterinarian can diagnose the condition with a simple test; treatment is with tear stimulants and artificial tear replacements. Because many cases are believed to result from an autoimmune response, in which the body destroys its own tear glands, the use of am immunosuppressive medication is one of the primary treatments. Other treatments, including surgery, are available for severe cases. The earlier the condition is caught, the better the chances for successful treatment; even so, most affected dogs will need lifelong treatment.

Progressive retinal atrophy is a hereditary disease in which the light-sensitive cells of the retina gradually die. Two types have been reported in Dachshunds. An early-onset type that develops before a year of age has been reported in miniature Long-haired Dachshunds. A later-onset (around 4 years of age) type has been reported in a variety of Dachshunds. Both types are probably recessively inherited. No treatment is effective.

Seizures

Seizures are not uncommon in dogs and may or may not have hereditary causes. Many environ-

Healthy eyes can come in different colors (Dapple).

mental factors can contribute to seizures, and often the cause is never determined. Epilepsy is usually diagnosed when a dog, especially a young dog, has repeated seizures for no apparent reason. Such dogs may have a hereditary form of epilepsy.

Seizures may be focal or generalized; the latter can be further subdivided into grand mal (convulsive) and petit mal (nonconvulsive). Generalized grand mal seizures are the type most commonly reported in dogs. They typically begin with the dog acting nervous, and then exhibiting increasingly peculiar behaviors (such as trembling, unresponsiveness, staring into space, and salivating profusely). This pre-ictal stage is followed by the ictal stage, in which the dog will typically stiffen, fall over, and paddle its legs and champ its jaws; the dog may also urinate, defecate, salivate, and vocalize. During this time the dog should be protected from injuries caused by hitting furniture or falling down stairs (wrapping it in a blanket can help secure it), and from other dogs (dogs will often attack a convulsing dog). The ictal stage usually lasts only a couple of minutes; if it continues for more than 10 minutes the dog should be taken to an emergency clinic. After the ictal stage, the dog will remain disoriented, may be temporarily blind, and will pant and sleep. This post-ictal stage may last from minutes to days. A veterinarian exam of the dog, including a complete history and description of the seizure onset and activity, should be performed as soon as possible.

"Ahh, I feel better now." Dogs that feel good are more likely to rest on their backs.

Diagnosis. No specific tests are available to confirm a diagnosis of epilepsy, although some abnormalities in the chemical composition of cerebrospinal fluid have been identified in some epileptic dogs. Dogs with recurrent seizures can be treated with phenobarbitol or, less commonly, potassium bromide to prevent them.

Because epilepsy is found more often in some breeds than others, including Dachshunds, and often runs in families, it is believed to have a hereditary component. In the breeds in which it has been studied most comprehensively, epilepsy appears to be inherited in a mode consistent with a single autosomal recessive allele (that is, a dog must inherit one copy of the responsible gene from each parent in order to

have epilepsy). Other evidence points to the probability that different genes cause epilepsy in different breeds, a situation that will delay a DNA test for it in all breeds.

Lameness

Lameness can occur because of injury or from hereditary skeletal problems. A veterinarian should examine any lameness that persists without significant improvement after 3 days of complete rest. Lameness associated with paralysis or back pain may indicate intervertebral disk disease (page 128) and should receive immediate attention.

Ice packs may help minimize swelling if applied immediately after an injury. The reduced tissue temperature lowers the metabolic rate and

Good health care is a lifelong commitment.

Passive motion can be important in preventing muscle contraction and maintaining the health of the joint in cases in which the limb must be rested. All movements should be slow and well within the joint's normal range of motion. Massage therapy can be useful for loosening tendons and increasing circulation.

Many injuries are quite painful and may require drug therapy for pain relief. Orthopedic surgeries can be particularly painful and almost always warrant analgesics. Pain has a self-perpetuating aspect, which means that it is easier to prevent than to stop. Discuss with your veterinarian the pros and cons of various analgesics.

Patellar Luxation

The dog's knee, or stifle, is the joint connecting the femur (thigh) bone to the tibia and fibula (shin) ones. The knee joint also contains three smaller bones, including the patella (kneecap). The patella's inner surface normally glides up and down within the trochlear groove of the femur as the knee flexes and contracts. It is also secured by the tendon of the quadriceps muscle as well as the surrounding joint capsule. In some dogs the groove may be too shallow, or the quadriceps exerts too much rotational pull, causing the patella to occasionally ride over the ridge of the trochlear groove when the knee is moving. When the patella is out of place (luxated) it usually can't return to its normal position until the quadraceps muscle relaxes.

inhibits edema and the sensation of pain. Cold therapy can be helpful for up to a week following an injury.

Heat therapy can be beneficial to older injuries. Heat increases the metabolic rate of the tissue, relaxes muscle spasms, and can provide some pain relief. Moist heat applied for about 20 minutes is preferable, although care must be taken to avoid burning.

Complete rest and total inactivity are the best initial home care for any lameness. Rest your dog well past the time she quits limping. Exercise therapy is equally as important, but exercise must be controlled. Leash walking and swimming are excellent low-impact exercises for recovering dogs.

Relaxing the quadraceps causes the leg to straighten at the knee, so the dog will often hop for a few steps until the patella pops back into place. As the patella pops both in and out of place, it causes some pain to the dog as it passes over the ridge of the trochlear groove, so some dogs may yelp. Depending on the severity of the condition, the patella may or may not pop back into place on its own. Four grades of patellar luxation severity are described:

• Grade 1: The dog may occasionally skip, holding one hind leg forward for a step or two. The patella usually stays in place, however, unless it is manually shifted out of position. It returns to its correct position easily.

• Grade 2: The dog often holds the affected leg up when running or walking, and the patella may not slide back into position by itself. When the leg is manipulated it has a grinding feeling.

• Grade 3: The patella is permanently out of position. Even when the patella is manually placed back in position, it doesn't stay long. The dog will some-times use the affected leg.

• Grade 4: The patella is always out of position and cannot be replaced manually. The dog never puts weight on the leg.

Patellar luxation gets gradually worse with age because every time the patella pops out of position it stretches the surrounding tissues that are needed to hold it into place and can even wear down the edge of the trochlear groove. The abnormal wear can lead to arthritic changes,

Dachshunds are stoic and often will not display pain.

which is one reason it's important to implement treatment early.

Many veterinarians consider surgery for Grades 2, and possibly 3, to be overkill, however, pointing out the discomfort, expense, and possible arthritic aftereffects of such surgery. Surgery may or may not be advised for Grade 3, but is almost always advised for Grade 4. In this procedure any stretched tissues are tightened and sutured, the groove may be reconstructed, and the quadriceps muscle may be realigned. A veterinary orthopedic surgeon has the special expertise needed to best perform this surgery.

Although the mode of inheritance is unknown, patellar luxation is con-sidered to have a strong hereditary component. Affected dogs should not be bred, and all breeding stock and their close relatives should be checked clear. The Orthopedic Foundation for Animals (OFA) maintains a registry for dogs that have been checked for patellar luxation.

Intervertebral Disk Disease

Intervertebral disk disease (IVDD) is the Dachshund's most well-known disorder. About a quarter of all Dachshunds will develop IVDD, occurring most often between 3 and 7 years of age. Most people erroneously attribute the condition to the Dachshund's long back, and in fact some European standards have been changed in response to protests from activists that the back must be shortened in relation to height to fight the condition. IVDD is not that simple, however.

Intervertebral disks are the cushions between the vertebrae of the spine. Each disk consists of a tough outer coating containing a gelatinous substance within. The gel substance in disks of dogs with dwarfism due to chondrodystrophy, such as Dachshunds, is abnormally fibrous and tends to become calcified, losing the elasticity needed to function as a shock absorber.

Disks work best at cushioning forces applied straight down the length of the back. They aren't as

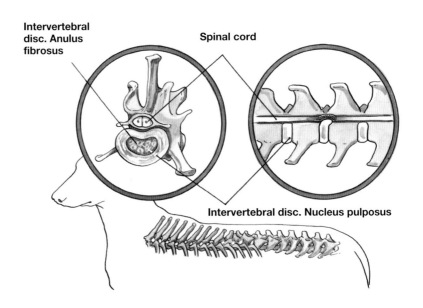

Intervertebral disc. Anulus fibrosus

Spinal cord

Intervertebral disc. Nucleus pulposus

The disks normally act as cushions between the vertebrae.

good at cushioning twisting forces because too much force is concentrated on only one part of the disk. The cumulative effect of twisting forces can weaken the outer covering and increase its chance of ripping. If that happens, the inner material squeezes into the area surrounding the spinal cord, compressing the cord.

Signs

Signs of disk herniation depend on location and severity. If it happens in the neck, the dog will usually have a painful neck. She may cry if it's moved, or she may walk with an arched back to keep it more level and less painful. Pain medication may help temporarily.

Most cases of IVDD occur in the lower back. Herniated disks here cause more damage because there is less extra space around the spinal cord. If the disk is slightly herniated the dog may walk with an arched back and stiff gait, and may cry when lifted. With increased herniation, she may drag her toes or have a wobbly gait, or, worse, her hind legs may become paralyzed and eventually lose pain sensation. The more severe the signs, and the longer the time before treatment is initiated, the worse the prognosis. The exception is that a dog with a chronic herniation has a better prognosis than one with an acute herniation of the same degree.

Although a presumptive diagnosis can be made based on clinical signs, a more definitive diagnosis requires

The eyes are the windows to the soul—keep them clear.

radiographs (X rays) and a myelogram. A radiograph allows the veterinarian to see displaced calcified material and abnormalities in the vertebral relationship, but it cannot pinpoint the exact location of the problem. A myelogram involves injecting a type of dye that shows up on radiographs into the cerebrospinal fluid. The veterinarian can see where the dye is diverted into an abnormal area and so pinpoint the site and estimate the severity of the herniation.

Treatment

Treatment depends on severity. More than half of patients with mild to moderate IVDD will recover at least temporarily with drug therapy

It's hard to slow an active Dachshund.

and rest. Drug therapy consists primarily of corticosteroids to reduce swelling and pain. Absolute cage rest is essential for 3 weeks beyond the time the dog appears well.

Extra care must be taken with dogs that cannot move, or are incontinent. The bed must be well padded with absorbent material to prevent bedsores. Any urine on the dog must be washed off to prevent urine scalding. Applying an ointment as a water barrier can be useful. The bladder may have to be manually expressed several times a day to prevent urinary tract infection.

Many owners too often feel sorry for their jailed Dachshund and let her run around earlier than they should in a misplaced act of kindness, causing

further damage. Even with optimal care, about 50 to 80 percent of these dogs will have subsequent episodes of IVDD during their lives unless surgery is also performed. Because of this, many veterinary neurologists believe surgery is the best course of treatment for all affected Dachshunds.

Dogs with recurrent episodes, or with more severe signs, such as weakness or inability to walk, should receive surgery. Such dogs are often in a great deal of pain even when confined to cage rest. Delaying surgery, especially in severe cases, decreases the chance of recovery and increases the chance of a sudden worsening of the problem with irreversible spinal cord damage. Although some partially paralyzed dogs can recover adequately on their own, it will take much longer and be less satisfactory than it would if surgery were performed. A completely paralyzed dog must have surgery within 48 hours or it will probably remain paralyzed.

Two types of surgery are routinely performed: decompressive surgery and fenestration. Decompressive surgery, in which any compressed masses of material around the spinal cord are removed, provides immediate relief and is very successful. It may be followed by fenestration, in which some of the gelatinous material from the disks is removed in order to prevent future disk herniation and pain at that site. Fenestration has some risks and drawbacks, including the possibility of infection, degenerative bony outgrowths (spondylosis), and redirected forces to other disks. If performed by an experienced surgeon who can minimize trauma, most veterinarians advocate fenestration as a preventive technique.

Recovering dogs should receive physical therapy in the form of gradual exercise. Swimming is ideal because it is nonweight bearing. Your Dachshund can learn to swim in your bathtub as you hold her in place. Special slings are available so you can support your dog's rear as she regains use of her legs. Dogs that drag their feet can damage them unless the feet are fitted with protective booties. Even exercise where your dog lies on her side or back and you manipulate her legs or encourage her to move them can be beneficial.

Not every dog recovers. Carts are available to support the dog's rear end so she can get around on her own. Carts are not a means of therapy, however, since the hind legs simply hang and get no exercise.

Prevention

Dachshund owners would prefer to prevent IVDD. One way is through breeding. Radiographs taken at about 18 months of age are advocated in order to look for calcifications of the disks, which correlate with the likelihood of developing IVDD later in life. A dog with one parent with calcification has a higher chance, and a dog with both parents with calcificiations an even higher chance, of developing calicifications than a dog with neither parent having them. Chances increase further with

Von Willebrand's Disease

Canine von Willebrand's Disease (vWD) is a hereditary deficiency in one of the clotting factors that can lead to excessive bleeding. Blood clotting depends not only on a sufficient number of platelets in the blood but also on a chain of chemical reactions of molecules known as clotting factors. Each successive factor in the chain reaction is identified numerically; in vWD factor VIII is abnormal or deficient. The degree of deficiency varies between affected individuals because of a somewhat randomized factor in the nature of the mutation that causes it. Dogs with only a slight deficiency will have few symptoms, but those with a greater deficiency may have prolonged or uncontrolled bleeding during surgeries or from cuts, lameness from bleeding into the joints, hematomas (accumulations of blood beneath the skin), nosebleeds, and other abnormal bleeding.

A simple blood test is available, but the results have a great deal of fluctuation. About 10 percent of this variability is from variations in the test itself, but most of the variation is due to variations within the dog's production of von Willebrand factor. This means that a dog with a suspicious test result should be retested several times before concluding that the dog is affected. Dachshunds have been diagnosed with vWD, but some breeders believe the diagnoses have been inaccurate.

increased numbers of calcifications in each parent. The evidence points to a hereditary factor, probably of a polygenic nature. This means that it does not depend on a single pair of genes, but instead on several genes all acting together in a cumulative fashion. Polygenic diseases are difficult to breed out of a population; it is critical to consider siblings of contemplated breeding stock as carefully as the direct ancestors when dealing with polygenic traits. That's why all Dachshunds, not just breeding stock, should be radiographed, as it gives breeders valuable family data. It's been advised that dogs with more than three calcifications should not be bred.

Although not documented, some dietary supplements may be of benefit to dogs at risk for IVDD. Vitamins E and C act as antioxidants and may help protect the cord if IVDD develops. Ginkgo biloba may be helpful in protecting the spinal cord after an injury. Foods rich in soy lecithin, such as tofu, may help support the myelin of the spinal cord. Preventing obesity and restricting jumping may help decrease the chance of disk herniation. Every Dachshund should be crate-trained so that if she needs cage rest she can endure it calmly.

First Aid

The time to prepare for an emergency is now. Have your veterinarian's emergency phone number at hand. Prepare a first aid kit; include a photocopy of these or other first aid instructions in it. Follow the directions outlined under the specific emergencies, call ahead to the clinic, and then transport the dog to get professional attention.

Your first aid kit should include
• Rectal thermometer
• Scissors
• Tweezers
• Sterile gauze dressings
• Self-adhesive bandage (such as Vet-Wrap)
• Karo syrup
• Instant cold compress
• Antidiarrheal medication
• Ophthalmic ointment
• Soap
• Antiseptic skin ointment
• Hydrogen peroxide
• Clean sponge
• Pen light
• Syringe
• Towel
• First aid instructions
• Veterinarian and emergency clinic numbers

Artificial Respiration

If your Dachshund isn't breathing, you may attempt artificial respiration.
• Open the mouth, clear the passage of secretions and foreign bodies, and pull the tongue forward.
• Seal your mouth over the dog's nose and mouth. Blow gently into the dog's nose for 2 seconds, and then release. Remember that Dachshunds have small lungs, so don't blow too hard or too long.
• If you don't see the chest expand, then blow harder, make a tighter seal around the lips, or check for an obstruction.
• Repeat at a rate of one breath every 4 seconds, stopping every minute to monitor breathing and pulse.
• If air collects in the stomach, push down just behind the rib cage every few minutes.

CPR

If your Dachshund's heart isn't beating, you may attempt cardiopulmonary resuscitation.

It's not unusual for an active Dachshund to get hurt, but it's up to you to keep her off her feet until she's fit.

• Place your finger tips from both hands, one on top of the other, on the left side of the chest about 1 inch up from and behind the point of the elbow.
• Press down quickly and release.
• Compress at a rate of about 100 times per minute.
• After every 15 compressions give two breaths through the nose. If you have a partner, the partner can give breaths every two or three compressions.

Heat Stroke

Early signs of heat stroke include rapid loud breathing, abundant thick saliva, bright red mucous membranes, and high rectal temperature. Later signs include unsteadiness, diarrhea, and coma.

Wet the dog down and place him in front of a fan. If this is not possible immerse the dog in cool water. *Do not plunge the dog in ice water;* the

Swimming is good therapy.

resulting constriction of peripheral blood vessels can make the situation worse. Offer small amounts of water for drinking.

You must lower your dog's body temperature quickly, but you don't want the temperature to go below 100°F. Stop cooling the dog when the rectal temperature reaches 103°F because it will continue to fall.

Even after the dog seems fully recovered, do not allow her to exert herself for at least 3 days following the incident. Hyperthermia can cause lasting effects that can result in death unless the dog is fully recovered.

Bleeding

Consider wounds to be an emergency if there is profuse bleeding, if they are extremely deep or large, or if they open to the chest cavity, abdominal cavity, or head.
• If possible, elevate the wound site, and apply a cold pack to it.
• Do not remove impaled objects; seek veterinary attention.
• Cover the wound with clean dressing and apply pressure. Don't remove blood-soaked bandages; apply more dressings over them and leave them even after bleeding stops.
• If the wound is on an extremity, apply pressure to the closest pressure point. For a front leg, press inside of the leg just above the elbow; for a rear leg, press inside of the thigh where the femoral artery crosses the thigh bone; for the tail, press the underside of the tail close to where it joins the body.

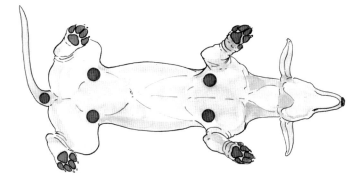

Apply pressure to the closest pressure point to slow bleeding.

• Use a tourniquet only in life-threatening situations and only when all other attempts have failed.

• For abdominal wounds, place a warm, wet sterile dressing over any protruding internal organs and cover with a bandage or towel. Do not attempt to push organs back into the dog.

• For head wounds, apply gentle pressure to control bleeding. Monitor for loss of consciousness or shock and treat accordingly.

• For animal bites, allow some bleeding, then clean the area thoroughly and apply antibiotic ointment. A course of oral antibiotics will probably be necessary. It's best not to suture most animal bites, but a large one (over 0.5 inch in diameter), or one on the face or other prominent position, may need to be sutured.

Snakebite

Poisonous snakebites are characterized by swelling, discoloration, pain, fangmarks, restlessness, nausea, and weakness. Most bites are to the head and are difficult to treat with first aid. The best first aid is to keep the dog quiet and to take her to the veterinarian immediately. Do not apply ice or tourniquets or attempt to make cuts on the wound. Antivenin is the treatment of choice.

Insect Stings and Allergic Reactions

Insects often sting dogs on the face or feet. Remove any visible stingers as quickly as possible by brushing them with a credit card or stiff paper; grasping a stinger often injects more venom into the dog. Administer baking soda and water paste to bee stings and vinegar to wasp stings. Clean the area and apply antibacterial ointment.

Call your veterinarian immediately if you think the dog may be having a severe reaction. Insect stings are the most common cause of extreme allergic reactions in dogs. Swelling around the nose and throat can block the airway. Other possible reactions include restlessness, vomiting, diarrhea, seizures, and collapse. If any of these symptoms occur, immediate veterinary attention will probably be necessary. Ask your veterinarian beforehand about keeping an antihistamine, such as Benadryl, on hand for such emergencies.

Chapter Twelve

Breeding Dachshunds of Distinction

Dachshunds are among the most beloved of all breeds, compelling many Dachshund owners to breed their dogs. As many reasons as there are to breed your dog, there are usually more reasons not to breed.

Why Breeding Is a Bad Idea

Good Homes Are Hard to Find

The popularity of Dachshunds may seem like one of the reasons in favor of breeding, but in fact it is not. More popular breeds actually have a more difficult time finding good, committed homes, instead attracting an unusually large percentage of impulse buyers who may be ill suited to own one. The Dachshund's popularity also attracts people with the wrong intentions, many of whom mistakenly believe they can make money by selling puppies. The pup you unwittingly sell them may live its life as a puppy-

To get the best, breed the best to the best—and hope for the best.

making machine, only to be discarded when the entrepreneur discovers how poor a business venture Dachshund breeding really is.

Good Homes

You want your puppies to find good homes. People who cared enough to do their homework to find good, responsible breeders are more likely to provide good homes. In other words, if you want to attract good homes, you need to be a good breeder. Responsible breeders have spent years researching genetics and the breed, breed only the best specimens that have proven themselves in competition, and screen for hereditary defects in order to obtain superior puppies. Unless you have done the same, you are doing yourself, your dog, the puppies, any buyers, and the breed a great disservice. Remember:

• Unless your Dachshund has proven herself by earning titles and awards, or comes from an impeccable background, you may have a difficult time finding good buyers.

• Your Dachshund should be free of hereditary disorders.

A bushel of mischief!

• Breeding dogs entails risks to the dam's life.

• Selling puppies will not come close to reimbursing you for the health clearances, stud fee, prenatal care, whelping complications, Caesarian sections, supplemental feeding, puppy food, vaccinations, advertising, and a staggering investment of time and energy.

Dachshund Genetics

If, despite all warnings, you're still contemplating breeding, be sure you breed the best dogs you can. It's assumed you've educated yourself about your dog's strengths and weaknesses, have a healthy female, and are familiar with Dachshund lines and studs. Your choice of breeding partners will affect the conformation, temperament, and health of your puppies. Great progress is being made in developing DNA tests and mapping the canine genome; meanwhile breeders must use what limited genetics information is currently available.

Dogs have two copies of each gene, which may or may not be the same as one another. A dominant gene only needs to be present in one copy in order that it be expressed; a recessive gene must be present in both copies to be expressed.

All dogs carry recessive genes for defects. Only when two dogs with the same defective recessive gene mate do they run the risk of producing affected offspring. The more closely two dogs are related, the higher the chance they will carry the same gene, and, if bred together, produce affected offspring. That's why it's generally safer to breed to as unrelated a partner as possible.

Many other traits are polygenic, that is, caused by the interaction of several sets of genes. These genes have an additive rather than all-or-none effect. Size is an example; breeding a small Dachshund to a large one won't just give you small and large Dachshunds, but will more likely give you a range, with many offspring intermediate in size. The extent of that range can often be estimated by the range in the sire's and dam's siblings. That's why it's important to consider both good and bad traits in siblings when looking at pedigrees.

Some breeders interbreed coat varieties and different sizes, but this is best left to experienced breeders. Breeding within a coat and size type will let you have a better idea of what to expect in your puppies.

Dachshund Disorders

The Dachshund's most vexing disorder, intervertebral disk disease, is probably polygenic. The chance of developing the disorder increases with the number of affected parents. Patellar luxation is also probably a polygenic disorder. Progressive retinal atrophy is a recessive disorder.

Coat Type

Wire coat is dominant to smooth coat, which is in turn dominant to long coat. The exact length and texture is further influenced by modifier genes.

Coat Color

Dachshund coat colors are determined by the distribution of two types of pigment: eumelanin (black) and phaeomelanin (red). Other genes determine whether any pigment is deposited at all, or how much it may be diluted. The following description includes only those genes for which more than one form have been demonstrated in Dachshunds; other breeds may have a different set of variable genes.

Let's start with the distribution of white. The **S** (white spotting) locus controls the amount of white, with variability in degree of spotting caused by each allele, perhaps due to modifiers or incomplete dominance.

Color breeding in Dachshunds can be a fascinating challenge.

- The **S** allele codes for no or very minor white markings.
- The **s^i** (Irish spotting) allele produces white neck, legs, tail tip, and perhaps underbody.
- The **s^p** (piebald) allele produces patched or spotted dogs.

The dominant **T** (ticking) allele allows for the formation of colored flecks to show through an otherwise white background. The recessive allele, **t**, produces a clear white background.

Color of spots and flecks reflect underlying color as though the white was poured over an otherwise colored dog. That color can occur in various patterns, hues, and intensities depending on the type of melanin and the presence of any dilution factors.

The **A** and **E** genes work together in determining the type of melanin present. The **E** series includes in order of dominance:

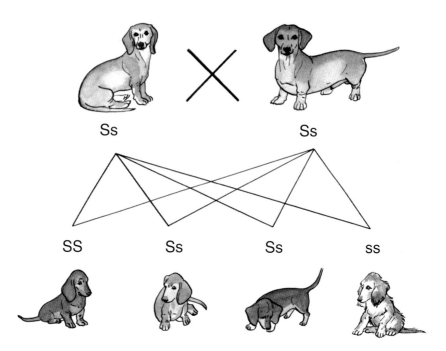

It's possible to get a Longhaired from two Smooth parents, but only if both parents carry a recessive Longhaired gene.

Ss × Ss

SS   Ss   Ss   ss

- The **E^br** (brindle) allele, which creates a pattern of irregular vertical dark stripes over a lighter background.
- The **E** allele, which allows for normal expression of whatever coat color is produced by alleles at the **A** series.
- The **e** allele, which allows the dog to produce only phaeomelanin (red) in the coat, although nose and skin pigment can have eumelanin (black).

The **A** series also controls the distribution of eumelanin versus phaeomelanin. Its alleles in order of dominance are **a^y**, **a^t**, and **a^w**.

- The **a^y** (sable) allele produces hair that is mostly tan or red with black tips or interspersed with black hairs. This accounts for black-fringed reds and reds that are born black and lighten into adulthood.
- The **a^t** (tan-point) allele produces tan-pointed dogs, typically black and tan, brown and tan, or blue and tan.
- The **a^w** (wild) allele produces agouti or wolf color in which the legs, face, and underside are light and each hair of the back and sides is banded with alternating light and dark pigment. This probably accounts for the wild boar pattern.

Eumelanin and phaeomelanin can exist in undiluted or in diluted forms,

Potential parents should be sound of body and mind.

depending on the influence of alleles at yet other locations.

The **B** locus has a dominant allele **B** that allows for undiluted eumelanin (black) and a recessive allele **b** that instead produces diluted eumelanin (chocolate) coat pigment and lighter nose, eye rim, and iris color.

The **C** locus has a dominant allele **C** that allows for undiluted color, and a recessive allele **c**^ch (chinchilla) that dilutes phaeomelanin and slightly dilutes eumelanin, producing a light tan coat color.

The **D** locus has a dominant allele **D** that allows for full black pigmentation and a recessive allele **d** that instead produces both diluted eumelanin and phaeomelanin, creating a gray or blue coat color as well as lighter skin and eyes.

The **M** (merle) locus has an incomplete dominant allele **M** (merling) and a recessive **m** (no merling). A single copy of **M** dilutes the coat in patches, interspersing areas of diluted and nondiluted coat. Eyes may be blue or partially blue. When two copies of **M** are present, large areas of white may also be created, as well as an increased chance of vision and hearing problems. The chance of other anomalies seems to be increased if the dog also has white due to the effects of the **S** series.

Breeding and Whelping

Arrangements should be made with the stud owner well in advance of the breeding. A written contract should spell out what expenses you'll be responsible for and what will happen if no puppies are born.

Estrus

Count the days from the first sign of bloody discharge, but don't rely on them to determine the right day to breed. If a lot is riding on the breeding, consider monitoring her estrus cycle by means of ovulation timing using blood samples. Vaginal smears can also give some guidance but are not nearly as reliable. An experienced stud dog is usually the most reliable indicator of the right time to breed, however. Most people breed the pair on alternate days for two to three breedings. Dogs ovulate all their eggs within 48 hours, so the idea that runts result from eggs fertilized from later breedings is not valid. AKC will register such puppies pending DNA paternity testing. This involves sending off samples from cheek swabs and can be expensive.

Gestation

Dachshund gestation averages 61 to 63 days from the date of the first breeding, but full-term gestation can range from 57 to 72 days. This variability results from the fact that fertile matings can occur well before and after the actual time of ovulation. To get a better idea of the due date, you should use a progesterone test during her heat cycle. From this your veterinarian can pinpoint the luteinizing hormone (LH) peak, which consistently occurs 64 to 66 days before whelping.

Pregnancy Determination

Around day 18 to 21 implantation occurs, and during this time some pregnant dogs will appear nauseous and even vomit. A skilled veterinarian can often determine the presence of fetuses by carefully feeling, or palpating, her abdomen at between 18 and 25 days of gestation. A canine pregnancy test (Reprochek) can detect the presence of relaxin, a substance produced by the placenta of a pregnant dog after implantation, typically by day 21 to 25 postfertilization. Human pregnancy tests don't work because, unlike in humans, even nonpregnant bitches have the same rise in the pregnancy hormones they detect as pregnant ones do. This is why dogs have pseudo-pregnancies; it's normal dog physiology because hormonally they are the same as dogs with real pregnancies.

By about day 35 pregnancy can be determined with ultrasound. Other signs that often develop by then are a mucous discharge from the vagina and enlarged, pinkish nipples. In the last week of pregnancy, radiographs can be used to count

Pyometra

Pyometra is a uterine infection that most commonly appears a month or two after estrus. Symptoms may include a mucous discharge from the vagina along with lethargy and fever. Contact your veterinarian immediately if you suspect pyometra; left untreated, it can be fatal. The best treatment is spaying, but medical drug therapy is sometimes successful for valuable breeding bitches.

Ticking (colored flecks on a white background, as in the dog on the left) is dominant over no ticking (as in the dog on the right).

fetal skeletons, but they are not always accurate. The knowledge of how many puppies to expect can be useful for knowing when the bitch has finished whelping.

The mother-to-be should be kept active throughout most of her pregnancy, but she should not be allowed to run and jump too vigorously as she nears her whelping date. She should begin to eat more, gradually switching to puppy food during the latter half of her pregnancy.

Whelping

Begin taking the expectant mother's temperature morning and evening every day starting about a week before the due date. When her temperature drops dramatically, to around 98°F (or 37°C) and stays there, you can anticipate pups within the next 12 hours. She will become increasingly restless and uncomfortable; eventually she will begin to strain with contractions.

The puppies are preceded by a water bag; once this has burst, the first puppy should be born soon. If a puppy appears stuck, you can use a washcloth and gently pull it downward (between her hind legs) along with her contractions. Never pull a puppy by a limb, tail, or head, though. You may wish to help the mother clear the pup's face so it can breathe, and you may wish to tie off the umbilical cord. Do this by tying dental floss around the cord about 0.75 inch (around 2 centimeters) from the pup, and then cutting the cord on the side away from the pup. Make sure that for every pup that comes out, a placenta comes out, too. Allow the dam to eat one placenta if she wants, as they contain important hormones, but they contribute to diarrhea and one is enough.

When to Get Help

You may have a whelping emergency if

• More than 24 hours have passed since her temperature dropped without the onset of contractions.

• More than 2 hours of intermittent contractions have passed without progressing to hard, forceful contractions.

• More than 30 minutes of strong contractions have passed without producing a puppy.

• More than 15 minutes have passed since part of a puppy protruded through the vulva and the puppy makes no progress.

• Large amounts of blood are passed during whelping.

Genes make the dog.

Postnatal Care of the Dam

A post-whelping exam is advisable to ensure that all pups and their placentas have been expelled. Sometimes a dead puppy is retained, causing a serious infection that often necessitates spaying.

Mastitis

Check the dam's mammary glands throughout nursing for signs of mastitis, which include pain, bloody discharge, and hard swelling. Home care includes hot compresses and gentle expression of the affected gland, while preventing pups from nursing from it. Call your veterinarian for advice; antibiotics may be necessary.

Eclampsia

One of the greatest dangers to Dachshund dams is the threat of eclampsia (puerperal tetany). It occurs when the amount of calcium lost in the milk is greater than the amount the body can absorb or produce. Eclampsia occurs most often during the first month of nursing, but it can also occur in late pregnancy. Smaller dogs, especially those with large litters that need a lot of milk, are predisposed.

Poor nutrition and improper supplementation can also contribute to the development of eclampsia. The optimal nutrition for the dam during the last half of her pregnancy and during nursing is a commercial puppy food. Because eclampsia occurs from too little calcium, many breeders try to avoid it by supplementing the dam with calcium during her pregnancy. However, this practice should be avoided because the excess calcium intake tends to decrease the body's efficiency in absorbing calcium from the diet and in mobilizing calcium from the bones—actually making eclampsia more likely. Supplementing with calcium during the first month of nursing, on the other hand, may be beneficial. You should discuss any supplementation with your veterinarian before implementing it, however.

Early signs of eclampsia include irritability, neglect of pups, and restlessness, followed by salivation, facial itching, stiffness, fever, increased heart rate, and loss of balance. Final signs are severe muscle contractions and seizures. Eclampsia is a medical emergency that needs immediate treatment if the dam is to survive. Emergency treatment involves slow intravenous administration of calcium; following this, the pups should be weaned as quickly as possible.

Neonatal Care

Newborns should have a regular respiration rhythm, a heart rate of more than 200 beats per minute, bright red gums, and a body temperature of 94 to 96°F. Dachshund birth weights range from about 6 ounces to 10 ounces. Birth weight does not correlate with adult weight.

Monitor the puppies to make sure they are getting milk; pups with cleft palates will have milk bubbling out of

Hernias

Umbilical hernias, in which the opening around the umbilical cord fails to close properly, are a common occurrence in dogs. Most hernias are small, and eventually only trap a small pocket of fat. Hernias in which the abdominal contents can be pushed in and out can pose the threat of eventually trapping and strangulating their contents and should be corrected surgically.

their nostrils as they nurse. During normal development, the two sides of the roof of the mouth grow together and fuse before birth, but in some pups they fail to do so. This leaves an opening between the oral and nasal cavities, creating a number of problems; however, it can often be corrected surgically. Both genetic and environmental factors probably play a role; some breeders claim that prenatal administration of folic acid lowers the incidence.

Weigh each pup on a gram scale daily. Although pups will likely experience a slight drop in weight the first day, after that they should steadily gain weight.

Puppies can't regulate their body temperature, and chilling can kill them. Never feed a chilled puppy. Maintain the temperature in part of the whelping box at about 85°F for the first week, 80°F for the second week, and 75°F for the third and fourth weeks. You can use a heat lamp over one part of the box or a heating pad in one small section. It is essential that the pups can crawl away from any heat source. Overzealous heating attempts will result in overheating and dehydration of the pups, which can have just as devastating effects as chilling.

Canine Herpes

Some neonates die for no apparent reason. Probably some of these are victims of canine herpes, a common infection passed mostly from respiratory secretions. Affected pups cry piteously and will not nurse. The herpes virus cannot replicate in high temperatures, and placing puppies in incubators at the first sign of symptoms has saved some. If you suspect canine herpes, keep your pups very warm and consult your veterinarian immediately.

Hand Rearing

Abnormally small pups or pups that lose weight may need supplemental feedings. If the dam has eclampsia or mastitis or is ignoring the pups, you will also probably need to supplement. It's a good idea to have some bitch milk replacement formula, available from your veterinarian, on hand before whelping. Dog milk is much richer than cow or other readily available milks, so it's best to buy formula specially formulated for dogs rather than trying to concoct your own. It's usually easier to tube-feed a newborn than it is to bottle-feed one, but bottle-feeding is more satisfying and should be attempted if possible. The pups

Testicle Descent

A fairly common defect of dogs is the failure of one or both testicles to descend normally into the scrotum. It's usually difficult to feel them in any puppy until a couple of weeks of age, but by 8 weeks you should be able to feel tiny testicles in a male's scrotum. Most are descended by 12 weeks, but some Dachshunds have been known to have very late descending testicles. After the age of 4 months, the chances of testicles descending are quite low.

should be fed every 2 hours for the first week or so of life, slacking off to every 3 hours once the pup has doubled its birth weight. The puppy must be stimulated to urinate and defecate after each feeding. This is done by rubbing the urogenital area and anus with a warm damp cloth, simulating licking by the dam.

Puppy Meets World

Puppies are born blind and deaf. The pigment is often not yet present on their nose, eye rims, and foot pads. If you plan to remove dewclaws, it should be done within the first 5 days. After that time, it is usually best to leave them as nature intended or to wait until the pup is older and can undergo anesthesia. Some disagreement exists on whether front dewclaws should be removed, but many breeders feel it prevents painful injuries later in life. Rear dewclaws, if present, should be removed.

Playtime!

The puppies' eyes will begin to open at around 10 days of age, and the ears at around 2 weeks. Around this time they will also start attempting to walk. Be sure to give them solid footing—not slippery newspaper!

Weaning

Introduce hungry pups to pureed food when they are about 3 weeks old. You may have to put a bit on their noses to get their tongues working and convince them this new substance is tasty. Some dogs catch on more quickly than others; don't worry if yours take a little longer. By about 4 to 6 weeks of age the dam will begin weaning them herself, and the pups will start to prefer solid foods.

Socialization

Few times are as fun as when the pups first venture out of the whelping box and begin to explore the world. Your job now is to make sure they are gradually exposed to new experiences without being exposed to danger or disease.

You want your pups to meet new people, but too often people carry with them communicable diseases. Never allow anyone into your home who has come from a place where dogs have gathered, such as a dog show or animal shelter, unless they at the very least remove their shoes and refrain from handling the puppies. Although you may seem like a less than perfect host, your pups' lives are too precious to take any chances

Nap time.

Questions to Ask Potential Buyers

• What are you looking for in a dog and why do you want a Dachshund?
• Have you had a Dachshund before? Where did you get any previous dogs, and what became of them?
• What activities have you pursued with other dogs, and what do you hope to pursue with your new Dachshund?
• Do you have sex, color, or coat preferences?
• What people and pets are in your family? How old are any children? Does everyone want a dog?
• Who will be the dog's primary caregiver?
• Do you own your home, live in a rental house, or in an apartment?
• Will the dog be left alone while you go to work? Where will the dog spend days? Nights?
• How will the dog be contained?
• How will the dog be exercised?
• Do you plan to obedience-train your dog?
• Do you plan to breed your dog? Have you bred other litters? What became of the offspring?
• Would you like to keep in contact with the breeder?
• Will you follow the breeder's advice about breeding the dog, whether male or female, even if that means neutering or spaying?
• If you are getting this dog for competition, what will happen if the dog doesn't turn out to be competitive, or when it retires?
• Will you abide by the breeder's contract?
• Do you have controversial ideas regarding any aspect of dog care?

"Hello world!"

with. See page 37 for a review of vaccinations and deworming.

The World Ahead

Most reputable Dachshund breeders prefer their puppies stay with them until they are at least 10 weeks of age. Your pups should be leash-trained and crate-trained before they go to new homes. They should have spent time away from their littermates. They should have had some car-riding experience and met men, women, and children. They should have stolen your heart in the process. If they haven't, you shouldn't be breeding.

Good breeders worry. They worry that the people who desperately want a puppy today will tire of it tomorrow. They worry that the cozy bedroom they described is really a pen in the garage. They worry that the motivations are not what they seem to be. Too many breeders have been burned by mistakenly placing their faith in the people who seemed ideal. You need to listen with a cautious ear to what you are told, watch carefully how the entire family interacts with your dogs, and ask many questions. Your puppies are depending on you to weed out homes that could become living nightmares; they are depending on you for the rest of their lives.

When you finally find a home worthy of your puppy, the hardest part of breeding a litter still awaits: saying good-bye to the puppies you've grown to love. If you're a good breeder, you'll keep in touch with their new families throughout their lives. You'll be there to answer questions, act as a safety net, hear of the latest antics, and commiserate as they grow old. If you're a good breeder, you'll be rewarded by the lives your puppies have brightened, and you'll have created an extended family of Dachshund lovers.

Chapter Thirteen
Long Lives

Old age is something to celebrate. It's the reward for good care, good genes, and good luck. It's a time of special sharing, special needs, and special memories.

Dachshunds have average to long lifespans of about 12 to 14 years, with some living well into their teens. Some Dachshunds seem youthful well into old age, but one day your playful puppy will be a senior, still saucy but a little bit calmer and wiser, still adventurous but a little bit slower and stiffer.

Venerable Veterans

Your geriatric Dachshund needs mental and physical stimulation but not at the level she did when younger. Lounging by your side, riding in the car, chomping down some treats, strolling around the block, racing around the house, greeting old friends, and barking at that squirrel she still plans to catch can fill an older dog's day.

The friend of a lifetime.

Your challenge is to stimulate your dog without overexerting or stressing him. Your dog may like car trips, but long trips can be taxing. Boarding may be even more stressful. Consider having a responsible house sitter stay with your dog if you must leave him. The house sitter should be familiar with your dog and any health problems she may have and should be well versed in Dachshund health and safety concerns.

If you haven't already arranged steps or platforms for your dog to get on and off furniture, be sure you do so now. Your Dachshund may not be able to jump up and down like she used to.

Older Dachshunds may be more susceptible to chilling in cold weather. They should have access to a warm, soft bed, and some may need to wear a sweater when going out in the cold.

Sensory Loss
Older dogs may experience hearing or visual loss. The slight haziness that appears in the older dog's pupils is normal and has minimal effect upon vision, but some dogs may

develop cataracts. These can be seen as almost white through the dog's pupils. Just as with people, severe cataracts can be removed and replaced with an artificial lens.

Dachshunds with hearing loss can learn hand gestures and also respond to vibrations. Dachshunds with vision loss can cope well as long as they are kept in familiar surroundings and extra safety precautions are followed. For example, block open stairways or pools, don't move furniture, and place sound or scent beacons throughout the house or yard to help the dog locate specific landmarks. Lay pathways, such as gravel or block walkways, outdoors, and carpet runners indoors.

Feeding

Keeping an older dog in ideal weight can be a difficult challenge. Both physical activity and metabolic rates decrease in older animals, so they require fewer calories to maintain the same weight. Excessive weight can place an added burden on the heart, back, and joints. However, very old dogs often tend to lose weight, which can be equally bad. Your dog needs a little cushion of fat so that she has something to fall back on if she gets sick.

High-quality protein is especially important for healthy older dogs. Most older dogs do not require a special diet unless they have a particular medical need for it. Older dogs should be fed several small meals and should be fed on time. Moistening dry food or feeding canned food can help dogs with dental problems enjoy their meals.

Grooming

Older dogs enjoy gentle brushing but not marathon grooming sessions. Regular brushing can help soothe dry, itchy skin by stimulating oil production. Older dogs tend to have a stronger body odor, but don't just ignore increased odors. They could indicate specific problems, such as periodontal disease, impacted anal sacs, seborrhea, ear infections, or even kidney disease.

Periodontal disease is a common problem. The dog may have bad breath, lick her lips constantly, be reluctant to chew, or even have swelling around the mouth. A thorough tooth cleaning, possibly combined with drug therapy, is necessary to relieve these dogs' discomfort.

Senior Health

Some older Dachshunds become cranky and impatient, especially when dealing with puppies or boisterous children. Don't just excuse such behavioral changes, especially if sudden, as due simply to aging. They could be symptoms of pain or illness.

The healthy older Dachshund should have a check-up twice a year. Blood tests can detect early stages of treatable diseases. The veterinarian can also detect heart murmurs that often develop with aging. The veterinarian will listen for abnormal

Taking time to smell the roses . . .

breathing sounds and feel for abnormal growths and, in intact males, an enlarged prostate gland.

Arthritis

Older dogs often suffer from arthritis, which causes intermittent inflammation, decreased range of motion, and pain. In some dogs there is no obvious cause. In others abnormal stresses or trauma to the joint can cause degeneration of the joint cartilage and underlying bone.

Conservative treatment entails keeping the dog's weight down, providing a soft warm bed, attending to injuries, and maintaining a program of exercise. Low-impact exercise such as walking every other day is best for dogs with signs of arthritis. Newer drugs, such as carprofen, are avail-

able from your veterinarian and may help alleviate some arthritic signs, but they should be used only with careful veterinary supervision. Some newer drugs and supplements may actually improve the joint. Polysulfated glycosaminoglycan increases the compressive resilience of cartilage. Glucosamine stimulates the synthesis of collagen and may help rejuvenate cartilage to some extent. Chondroitin sulfate helps to shield cartilage from destructive enzymes.

Illness

Older dogs may have less efficient immune systems, making it increasingly important to shield them from infectious diseases, chilling, overheating, and stress. At the same time, an older dog that is never

Hyperadrenocorticism (Cushing's Syndrome)

Middle-aged or older Dachshunds are particularly prone to Cushing's syndrome, in which the body produces too much of the hormone cortisol. This usually happens because of a nonmalignant tumor on the pituitary gland in the brain or, less often, a tumor on the adrenal glands. The overstimulation with cortisol produces a variety of signs including increased hunger, thirst, and urination, as well as hair loss, muscle atrophy, lack of energy, and a pot-bellied appearance.

Several screening tests are available. A normal urine cortisol-to-creatinine ratio usually indicates that a dog doesn't have hyperadrenocorticism; an abnormal ACTH stimulation test suggests that the dog does have it. Treatment is usually with drugs, which must be continued throughout the dog's life.

Although a hereditary mechanism has not been identified, the prevalence of hyperadrenocorticism in some breeds suggests a genetic component in at least these breeds. Affected dogs should not be bred.

exposed to other dogs may not need to be vaccinated as often or for as many diseases as a younger dog. This is an area of current controversy that you should discuss with your veterinarian.

Vomiting and diarrhea in an old dog can signal many different problems, some of which can be serious. An older Dachshund cannot tolerate the dehydration that results from continued vomiting or diarrhea, so you should never let it continue unchecked. In general, any ailment that an older dog has is magnified in severity compared to the same problems in a younger dog.

Dogs suffer from many of the same diseases of old age that humans do. Cancer accounts for almost half of all deaths in dogs over 10 years of age. Some signs of cancer are abnormal swellings that don't go away or that continue to grow; loss of appetite or difficulty eating or swallowing; weight loss; persistent lameness; bleeding; collapse; or difficulty breathing, urinating, or defecating. Most of these symptoms could also be associated with other disorders, so that only a veterinary examination can determine the real problem.

A Promise Kept

You promised your dog you would care for her always, giving her the best quantity and quality of life you could. At some point you won't be able to give her both quantity and quality. No matter how hard you try, you will eventually face a disease you can't beat and have to weigh quantity versus quality. If your dog never wants to walk or eat, or if she is fighting for her breath or in pain, you should talk to your veterinarian about her chances of improvement.

We all wish that if our dog has to go, she would fall asleep and never awaken. This, unfortunately, seldom happens. Even when it does, you are left with the regret that you never got to say good-bye. The closest you can come to this is with euthanasia. Euthanasia is painless and involves giving an overdose of an anesthetic. Essentially the dog will fall asleep and never awaken.

Senior Dachshunds have their special charm.

Symptoms and Some of Their Possible Causes in Older Dogs
• Diarrhea: kidney or liver disease; pancreatitis
• Coughing: heart disease; laryngeal paralysis; lung cancer
• Difficulty eating: periodontal disease; oral tumors
• Decreased appetite: kidney, liver, or heart disease; pancreatitis; cancer
• Increased appetite: diabetes; Cushing's syndrome
• Weight loss: heart, liver or kidney disease; diabetes; cancer
• Increased urination: diabetes, kidney or liver disease; cystitis; Cushing's syndrome
• Limping: arthritis; patellar luxation;intervertebral disk disease
• Nasal discharge: tumor; periodontal disease
• Collapse: heart disease; internal bleeding; hypoglycemia
• Incoordination: intervertebral disk disease; vestibular syndrome; stroke

If you do decide that euthanasia is the kindest farewell gesture for your beloved friend, discuss with your veterinarian beforehand what will happen. You may ask about giving your dog a tranquilizer beforehand, or having the doctor meet you at home. Although it won't be easy, try to remain with your dog so that her last moments will be filled with your love. Try to recall the wonderful times you have shared and realize that however painful losing such a once-in-a-lifetime friend is, it is better than never having had such a partner at all.

Grief
Some people mark the passing of a dog with little emotion. For others, the dog is their best friend and surro-

gate child, perhaps the most important being in their lives. They often face the loss of their dog with little support from others. Coming to terms with losing a dog who is so vital to your happiness is one of

Sharing your heart is the best way to mend it.

the most difficult challenges many people will ever face. Yet one day you will have to meet that sad challenge. Denial is the first reaction you may have to the news your dog has a terminal illness. It's a natural reaction that protects us from the emotional impact of the painful truth. The next reaction is anger—anger that dogs live so short a time, anger that the treatments for humans are not available to dogs, and even anger at those who have older dogs. Anger eventually becomes depression, when the truth is accepted and the futility of fighting acknowledged. Depression can begin well before actually losing a dog, and last well after. It can involve such a feeling of helplessness and defeat that a person may not even try some reasonable therapies for their dog. Although depression is natural, protracted depression can be extremely damaging. Pet bereavement counselors are available at many veterinary schools.

The last stage of grief is acceptance. Accepting the loss of a loved one doesn't mean you don't care; it just means that you realize that you have to do so in order to continue living and loving again. A new Dachshund will never take the place of your old dog, but it can provide a much-needed distraction and a target for your love. Sharing your heart is the best way to mend it.

Dachshund Resources

Organizations

Dachshund Club of America
Andra O'Connell, Secretary
1793 Berme Road
Kerhonkson, NY 12446
(845) 626-4137
http://www.dachshund-dca.org
(This site also links to International
Dachshund clubs.)

National Miniature Dachshund Club
http://dachshund-nmdc.org/

North American Teckel Club
http://www.teckelclub.org

List of Regional Dachshund Clubs
http://dachshund-dca.org/clubs.html

German Dachshund Club
(Deutscher Teckelklub)
http://www.dtk1888.de

American Kennel Club (AKC)
5580 Centerview Drive
Raleigh, NC 27606-3390
(919) 233-9767
http://www.akc.org

Canadian Kennel Club
89 Skyway Avenue, Suite 100
Etobicoke, Ontario M9W 6R4
(800) 250-8040
http://www.ckc.ca

United Kennel Club (UKC)
100 East Kilgore Road
Kalamazoo, MI 49001-5593
(616) 343-9020
http://www.ukcdogs.com

Other National All-breed Kennel Clubs
http://henceforths.com/kennel_clubs. htm

Canine Health Foundation
http://www.akcchf.org

Canine Eye Registration Foundation (CERF)
1248 Lynn Hall, Purdue University
West Lafayette, IN 47907
(765) 494-8179
http://www.vet.purdue.edu~yshen/ cerf.html

American Working Terrier Association
http://www.dirt-dog.com/awta

Orthopedic Foundation for Animals
2300 E. Nifong Blvd.
Columbia, MO 65201
(573) 442-0418
http://www.offa.org

National Animal Poison Control
  Center
(800) 548-2423
http://www.napcc.aspca.org/

Home Again Microchip Service
1-800-LONELY-ONE

Therapy Dogs International
88 Bartley Road
Flanders, NJ 07836
(973) 252-9800
http://www.tdi-dog.org

Rescue
Almost Home Dachshund Rescue
  Society
http://www.almosthomerescue.org/

Dachshund Adoption and Rescue:
http://www.daretorescue.com

Dachshund Rescue of North America
http://www.drna.org

Dachshund Rescue Web Page:
http://www.drwp.net

Periodicals
AKC Gazette
http://www.akc.org

Dog World Magazine
www.dogworldmag.com

Animal Network
http://www.animalnetwork.com

Books
Adamson, Eve. *Dachshunds for Dummies.* New York: Hungry Minds, 2001.

Coile, D. Caroline. *Beyond Fetch: Fun Interactive Activities for You and Your Dog.* New York: Wiley, 2003.

Coile, D. Caroline. *Encyclopedia of Dog Breeds.* Hauppauge, NY: Barron's Educational Series, 1998.

Coile, D. Caroline. *Show Me! A Dog Showing Primer.* Hauppauge, NY: Barron's Educational Series, 1997.

Gordon, Ann. *The Dachshund: A Dog for Town and Country.* New York: Howell, 2000.

Hutchinson, Dee and Bruce. *The Complete Dachshund.* New York: Howell, 1997.

Meistrell, Lois. *The New Dachshund.* New York: Howell, 1976.

Palika, Liz. *The Complete Idiot's Guide to Dachshunds.* New York: Alpha, 2002.

Pinney, Chris. *Dachshunds: Everything About Purchase, Care, Nutrition, and Behavior.* Hauppauge, NY: Barron's Educational Series, 2000.

Videos
AKC Breed Standard Video
http://www.akc.org/store/

Web Pages
Animal CPR
http://members.aol.com/henryhbk/acpr.html

Born to Track (Blood Trailing)
http://www.born-to-track.com

The Dachshund Network
http://www.thedachshundnetwork.com

Disabled Dachshund Society
http://new.rushmore.com/~dds/

Dachshund Circus
http://www.dachshundcircus.com

Dachshund.org (DORG)
http://www.dachshund.org

For the Love of Dachsies
http://www.dachsie.org

Dachshunds on the World Wide Web
http://www.standifird.net/wwwdachs/

"Which way did he go?"

Clicker Solutions
http://www.clickersolutions.com

The Dog Agility Page
http://www.dogpatch.org/agility/

The Dog Obedience and Training Page
http://www.dogpatch.org/obed/

Dr. P's Dog Training Links
http://www.uwsp.edu/acad/psych/dog/dog.htm

Infodog Dog Show Site
http://www.infodog.com

Index